# Hearts of Courage

The Gillam plane crash
and the amazing true story
of survival in the frozen
wilderness of Alaska

## John M. Tippets

PO Box 221974 Anchorage, Alaska 99522-1974
books@publicationconsultants.com
www.publicationconsultants.com

ISBN 978-1-59433-077-3

Library of Congress Catalog Card Number: 2008928492

—Second Edition—

Cover Painting and Maps by Terry Pyles

www.alaskanart.net

Printed in USA

For Joe and Alta

*Be of good courage, and he shall strengthen
your heart, all ye that hope in the Lord.*

*Psalm 31:24*

# Contents

*Alta and Joseph Tippets, Anchorage, Alaska.*

# FOREWORD

Joseph Henderson Tippets was born in Arimo, Idaho, on December 11, 1913. He was the youngest of eight, with seven older sisters. Their father had a small hotel and livery stable in Arimo, but soon gave it up to take a job with the Union Pacific Railroad. Joe then spent his early years in Ogden, Utah, and Cheyenne, Wyoming, where his father was a stationmaster. When his father died suddenly in 1926, Joe and his mother lived for a few years in California and later in Helper, near Price, Utah. The nation was in the midst of the "great depression" and their circumstances were very humble. After Joseph graduated from high school, he set his sights on joining the U.S. Navy. His first visit to Alaska was as a radio operator on the USS *San Francisco,* when it made port at Dutch Harbor in 1935.* "Too cold!" he wrote his mother.

*The USS *San Francisco* was participating in the navy's Fleet Problem XVI, an early and limited recognition that, if a war with Japan might occur in the future, the North Pacific and the Aleutian Islands would be critical in the defense of Alaska and of the North American mainland.

That same year, he renewed his acquaintance with Miss Alta Mahoney of Heber Valley, Utah. Alta's older brother, Vestus, was married to Joe's sister, Mary. Alta's parents did not view her long-distance romance with a young sailor favorably, so Joe and Alta eloped in September 1936.

Joe stayed in the navy for another year and then, in 1937, started his career with the Bureau of Air Commerce. In 1938, it became part of the Civil Aeronautics Authority, then two years later, the Civil Aeronautics Administration (CAA).* After seven eventful years in Alaska (1940-1947), he was promoted to CAA Headquarters in Washington, D.C.

In early January 1943, on a snow-covered mountain in Southeast Alaska, the lives of Joseph and Alta Tippets were changed forever. The "Gillam Crash" of the Morrison-Knudsen Electra, on which Joe was a passenger, was well known to aviators in Alaska. Harold Gillam was a celebrated bush pilot. The challenging winter of '42-'43 was described as the coldest recorded in thirty years, and the inspiring accounts written by the survivors have stirred the hearts of many. It is a true Alaska adventure story—a struggle against all odds to overcome the wilderness and ultimately find rescue.

It was an ordeal that required the greatest possible faith and courage. Marshal C. Hoppin, the first CAA Regional Administrator in Alaska, wrote in March 1943, "The fact that even four onboard the ill-fated plane survived the long, miserable month almost taxes our imagination, and proves indeed that faith, hope, courage, and endurance have tangible rewards. The age of miracles is not yet past!"[1]

---

*The Civil Aeronautics Authority was separated into two organizations in 1940, the Civil Aeronautics Board (CAB) and the Civil Aeronautics Administration (CAA). In 1958, the Federal Aviation Agency (FAA) was created.
[1] *The Mukluk Telegraph*, March 1943.

Terry Pyles

*The Northwest, from Seattle to Alaska.*

# ACKNOWLEDGEMENTS

In their lives together, Joseph and Alta Tippets shared many blessings and were grateful for them. The dramatic events of January and February 1943, involving an Alaska plane crash, weeks of anxious prayer, and Joseph's strong determination to survive, ultimately resulted in a joyful reunion and their renewed dedication to each other and the future.

Although the story of the Gillam plane crash has been described in various publications over the years, it has long been my hope to be able to pull together new details and recollections, including letters and documents that would provide a more complete account of the event. I first glimpsed the crash site from the air in the summer of 1963 while working as an engineer's aide on Annette Island, Alaska. In 1984, my brother, David, my oldest son, Joe, and I were fortunate to be able to accompany a team from Ketchikan who were attempting to recover one of the engines of the Lockheed Electra 10-B for museum exhibits in Ketchikan and Fairbanks. Gradually, the wreckage is sinking further into a small ravine on the side of the mountain, but it was still visible when my wife and I flew over it in August 1998. Boca de Quadra is a remote and beautiful inlet on the coast of Southeast Alaska, now part of the Misty Fjords National Monument.

The specific sources that have been most helpful to me in writing *Hearts of Courage* are listed in "Resources" at the back of the book and include some recently published materials. Of the new items, three are of particular interest: The U.S. Forest Service and TIGHAR 2004 site examination, a condensed version of which is included on pages 131-141; an article in the December 2004 *TIGHAR Tracks,* "The Men Did Their Duty: The Story of the Ketchikan Electra Crash," by Arthur Rypinski, an excellent piece, especially about the recovery of Robert Gebo and Dewey Metzdorf; and the 2005 biography of Harold Gillam, *Bush Pilot,* by Arnold Griese.

I express my thanks to all who have helped me in writing my parents' story. Many friends and family members have generously shared letters, photos, and personal memories. Much credit goes to Don "Bucky" Dawson of Ketchikan for his efforts, along with pilot Dale Clark, in relocating the crash site in 1981 and for his continued interest and research. In addition to his work on museum exhibits and presentations in Ketchikan and Fairbanks, Alaska, Don also gave a special presentation about Harold Gillam and the crash at the Smithsonian Air and Space Museum in Washington, D.C. in 1988. I am also grateful to Richard Van Cleave, senior curator of collections for the

Ketchikan Museums; the Alaska Aviation Heritage Museum; Martin V. Stanford, U.S. Forest Service archeologist; Richard Gillespie of The International Group for Historic Aircraft Recovery; Glen Rowe, historian with the L.D.S. Church Archives; and Hall Anderson and Chip Porter, who took photographs for me in Boca de Quadra in 2006 and

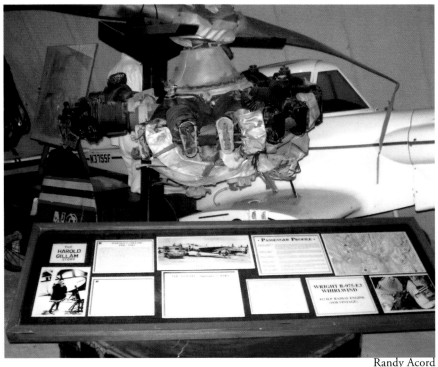

Randy Acord

*"The Harold Gillam Story" Exhibit prepared by Don Dawson on display at Fairbanks Alaskaland Pioneer Air Museum.*

2007, respectively. Additional thanks go to the family of Susan Batzer and to the artists who have provided wonderful illustrations: Terry Pyles, for the cover painting, Hubbard Glacier, and maps; David Draper for "Surviving the Crash;" Martin Stanford for the Tongass National Forest map; and David Rubin, for the "*Tucsan* Rescue." My special appreciation to Trudy Johnson, who has enthusiastically taken on the ramblings and revisions of multiple drafts, and to Susan Drake and Kathy Fryske, who have helped with correspondence and presentations to airline and credit union audiences. I am grateful for Marthy Johnson and Evan Swensen for meticulous editing and valued direction in the publishing process, and for their critique, comments and suggestions, I am similarly grateful for the input of many others who have read various drafts. And I especially thank my wife, Bonnie, for her editing and loving encouragement. Without her understanding and support, this project would not have been possible.

Finally, I am deeply grateful to my parents, Joseph and Alta, for their lives and good examples. I hope these chapters will convey my appreciation for their love, courage, determination, and faith.

*John M. Tippets*
*February 2008*

*Hubbard Glacier near Yakutat, Alaska.*

# INTRODUCTION

## CHRISTMAS 1942

*"It would be one of her last happy moments for many weeks."*

With great excitement and anticipation, Joe and Alta arrived in Alaska during the summer of 1940 for his new job with the Civil Aeronautics Administration. Three years earlier, Joe had transferred from the Navy to begin his career as a radio operator with the Bureau of Air Commerce in Wendover, Utah. Now his assignment was at Yakutat on the coast of Southeast Alaska, 200 miles north of Juneau and about 370 miles southeast of Anchorage. Because of the vast distances and the limitations of radio technology, it was necessary to maintain a series of signal relay stations across the territory. Yakutat was one of those locations.

Alaska and British Columbia, Canada, have majestic glaciers and towering mountains in this region of North America. It was beautiful country, but somewhat isolated. The inhabitants of Yakutat in 1940 included about 250 native members of the Tlingit Indian tribe, 20 local trappers and fishermen, and 97 CAA, weather bureau, and PNA airline employees as well as U.S. Coast Guard personnel.

Aircraft operations were still on the bay, but a site had been chosen for an airstrip. By mid-1940, construction was underway and by

November, the first planes were landing. The construction workers were mostly housed in temporary barracks.

Joe's next job was as a radio electrical engineer at the CAA regional office in Anchorage. He and Alta were glad for the change of pace. Military activity was accelerating all over Alaska. Fort Richardson was well established at Anchorage and the new Elmendorf Army Airfield was completed in September 1940. The population was booming and housing was in short supply. With a new addition to their family, baby John, they decided to build a home of their own. Thanks to help from friends and coworkers, their house on I Street, between Eleventh and Twelfth avenues, was soon finished.

*Johnny and Alta.*

A few months later, in the spring of 1941, the first local congregation of the Church of Jesus Christ of Latter-day Saints was organized in Anchorage. Several LDS (Mormon) families had settled in the area in additional to about a dozen LDS servicemen from western states assigned to Fort Richardson and Elmendorf. Joseph Tippets was asked to serve as the lay leader, or "branch president," for the group. The little house on I Street became a popular spot for Sunday dinners and social gatherings.

*Joseph and Alta Tippets' home, 1941-1943.*

*Anchorage Branch President Joseph Tippets, with LDS servicemen, 1941.* *

*LDS Anchorage Branch, Mother's Day, 1941.*

Suddenly, on December 7, 1941, Japan attacked Pearl Harbor on the island of Oahu and Alaska was immediately put on war footing.

*Servicemen in the branch at that time included Captain Harold Johnson, W. René Richardson, Morris Decker, Don Anderson, Charles "Chick" Hailes, Allan Eriksen, Jack Earington, Omer J. Smith, Lewis Smith, Harold Goff, Jack Arrington, and Melvin J. Hogan.

Price controls were initiated, many items were rationed, and black-outs were strictly enforced. Most travel was restricted and mail to and from Alaska was inspected by a censorship board set up in Seattle. The wife of a construction supervisor, trying to correspond with the Morrison-Knudsen employee newsletter, described her "blast from Seward's icebox—we are limited in the scope of our communications (we cannot even describe the weather here!) and no picture-taking. I hope I can work out something creditable to report."* It was almost

Anchorage Museum of History and Art
*Anchorage 4th Avenue, early 1940s.*

impossible to get permission to come into the territory from Canada or the lower 48 unless you were military or a government employee.

In June 1942, the Japanese bombed Dutch Harbor in the Aleutians and captured two small islands, Attu and Kiska, near the western end of the Aleutian chain. These attacks were part of their strategy to capture Midway Island (which was unsuccessful) and provide forward positions where they could detect and defend against any American advances in the North Pacific.

*The Em Kayan, 1942.

During the next twelve months, U.S. forces urgently mounted naval, air, and finally, infantry actions to drive the Japanese from American soil. The Aleutian campaign had to be fought not only against the enemy, but also against the extreme weather—ice, rain, fog and bitter cold. For many days in the winter months, the two sides would be totally unable to see each other. Hundreds of U.S. planes were lost, but only a few to enemy guns. By spring 1943, the U.S. Navy had largely blocked Japanese troop and supply ships from reaching the islands. The subsequent infantry assault on Attu in May resulted in devastating casualties,* but successfully ended Japan's occupation of Attu and Kiska.

Soon after Dutch Harbor was bombed in 1942, rumors and speculations spread concerning possible additional attacks on Alaska. There were radar reports of a Japanese task force in the North Pacific and a Pearl Harbor intercept suggested a possible invasion of the small gold-rush town of Nome, the mainland's western-most settlement of any size. The Alaska military command, headed by Brigadier General Simon Buckner, quickly launched "Operation Bingo" to beef up Nome's defenses. Over two thousand men, twenty anti-aircraft guns, plus ammunition and logistical support, were soon being airlifted the 580 miles from Anchorage by a steady stream of military and commercial aircraft that the general had commandeered for the effort. Communications were also essential and five emergency radio stations were soon in place. Navy and Army Air Corps planes patrolled the seas off Nome continuously for a month. But, by the Fourth of July, with no further indication of a Japanese threat, the airlift was ended. This false alarm, however, prepared Nome for a future significant role in the war, one which would continue for the next three years.

Beginning in September 1942, Nome was going to be the key to the Alaska-Siberia air route for the lend-lease aircraft going to the Soviet Union. Bombers and other types of military planes built in the U.S.

*The battle for Attu claimed 512 American and 2,350 Japanese lives. By August 1943, all of the Aleutians were under full control of the U.S. military.

17

were flown by American pilots along a route from Great Falls, Montana to Edmonton and Whitehorse in Canada, and on to Ladd Field at Fairbanks. Soviet pilots then took over and flew the planes to Galena and then Nome, Alaska, the last stop before heading to Siberia. For the pilots, especially the Soviets, it was a difficult and dangerous job.

The Nome airfield, on the southern coast of the Seward Peninsula, had originally been built by the CAA, but was rapidly being expanded to accommodate the A-20 light bombers, P-32 and P-39

Library of Congress

*P-39 fighter in Nome, Alaska before taking off for Siberia.*

fighters, and similar aircraft heading west. The previous year had not been encouraging for the American and Allied forces as they struggled against the enemy on two fronts.

By December 1942, Joe Tippets was on assignment at Nome updating radio equipment. He marveled at the sight of the Aurora Borealis, even though these "northern lights" often caused disruption in the short wave signals. There were only a few hours of daylight this far north and the weather was extremely cold. Temperatures of sixty below were not unusual and icy winds off the Bering Sea made his work especially challenging. The control tower was preparing for an incoming flight of A-20s when Joe received an urgent message from his wife in Anchorage. His mother down in Utah was seriously ill and not expected to recover. His sisters were asking, "Could he come? Could he come soon?" Not an easy question to answer from Nome, Alaska, in the middle of a war. But he would try. As soon as he could arrange it, he grabbed a seat on the next CAA plane heading south. The following day, he was back in Anchorage. But, how to tell Alta he would be gone over Christmas? Another baby was on the way and he knew how much she missed her family in Heber. He didn't relish leaving Alta and little Johnny, but he was his mother's only son and felt he should try to be with her one last time. Friends promised to stay close and Joe's niece, Mildred Hackett, who had recently taken a job with the CAA in Anchorage, decided to move into their little house for the duration. Mildred would be a great comfort in the coming weeks.

It was Monday, December 21, when space became available on one of the Morrison-Knudsen company planes bound for Seattle. Joe's supervisor gave him some reports to deliver to the Seattle CAA office, which made his trip "official government business."

"Hurry back, Darling!" Alta anxiously kissed her husband good-bye as he left from Merrill Field, the civilian airport at Anchorage. She wanted to be supportive, but it was hard not to worry. Air travel in Alaska was always a little risky, but especially so in the winter. As it turned out, the M-K plane did experience some engine problems a few hours into the flight, but Joe decided it would be better not to mention it to Alta.

Once in Seattle, the plan was to go by train to Ogden, Utah, thirty miles north of Salt Lake City. His mother, Josephine Tippets, had been at home in Ogden being cared for by three of his sisters, but was now in the hospital. The days went by quickly. She recognized Joe, but several strokes had left her partially paralyzed and unable to speak. It was hard seeing her in such fragile condition. He was grateful he had made it home in time.

Meanwhile, back in Anchorage, Alta was doing her best to make the holidays special. With help from two young soldiers from Ft.

Richardson, she and Mildred put up a small spruce tree and decorated it with some colorful ornaments Alta's mother had sent. Under the tree on Christmas morning were a few wrapped presents and a toy car for Johnny. They missed Joe, but later that day several friends came by to keep them company. In Alta's words, "It would have been a dreary Christmas if it hadn't been for the soldier boys and our friends from church." Each guest brought something to share so they were able to enjoy quite a nice dinner. Alta didn't know it then, but it would be one of her last happy moments for many weeks.

By New Year's Eve, Joe was on his way back to Seattle. He had spent a day in Heber visiting Alta's family and was then able to meet with several Church officials in Salt Lake City, including Elders Nicholas G. Smith, J. Reuben Clark, and David O. McKay. Elder Smith had been the LDS mission president assigned to Alaska when Joe was called to be the branch president. He also met with some of the parents of the young servicemen in his Anchorage Branch and he wrote to Alta, "Sweetheart, all the mothers think it is just wonderful the way you are looking out for their boys and they each express their thanks. Alta, I miss you and love you! I thank God for having you as my wife and, needless to say, I haven't been able to get you and Johnny out of my thoughts. Godspeed our quick reunion and I hope I beat this letter to you!"

Joe couldn't foresee what the future was about to bring or how many desperate days would go by before he and Alta would be together again.

Author's note: The following chapters of *Hearts of Courage* are written in my father's words, as described in news accounts, taped interviews, and other published resources. This is his story as he experienced it in January and February 1943.

*Harold Gillam, bush pilot, in front of Stearman aircraft on skis, early 1930s.*

Chapter One
# HAROLD GILLAM, BUSH PILOT

*"One engine has conked out, expect trouble."*

We were all looking forward to happier times in 1943. Heading back to Alaska, I made my way from Salt Lake City to Portland, Oregon, spending a few hours on January 4 visiting with Desla Bennion, the leader of the Northwestern States LDS Mission. From there, I continued on to Seattle, where I completed some CAA business and confirmed arrangements to catch a flight north to Anchorage the next day. I would be one of five passengers on board a Morrison-Knudsen aircraft. The Morrison-Knudsen Company, based in Boise, Idaho, was a major contractor in Alaska with a number of wartime projects for the army and the CAA. To support their widespread activities, they maintained a fleet of fifteen airplanes of various descriptions. The particular plane scheduled to fly to Anchorage on January 5 was a Lockheed Electra 10-B (NC 14915), piloted by M-K's chief pilot, Harold Gillam. Harold had flown this aircraft almost exclusively since Morrison-Knudsen had acquired it the previous year.

The Electra was a twin-engine monoplane, originally configured for ten passengers, but in this aircraft, two seats had been removed to make room for an auxiliary gas tank. When launched in 1934, the Electra was Lockheed's first all-metal design. Its length was about 39 feet, its wingspan 55 feet, and it had a maximum speed of 202 miles per hour. With a fully enclosed, pressurized cabin and extensive instrumentation, it was a very modern plane for that era. It was a similar Electra that Amelia Earhart had been piloting on her 1937 attempt to circumnavigate the globe.

Morrison-Knudsen *Em Kayan* Publication
*Three aircraft of the Morrison-Knudsen fleet.*

Morrison-Knudsen *Em Kayan* Publication
*Lockheed Model 10-B Electra NC-14915 piloted by*
*Harold Gillam at Merrill Field, Anchorage, Alaska, 1942.*

Air transportation had become essential to Alaska even before World War II. In the 1920s and '30s, the "bush pilots," men and women who flew in backcountry Alaska, had many stories of daring rescues and tragic crashes. These were part and parcel of Alaska aviation. Charles Harold Gillam was one of those very famous pilots who had been flying primitive, but constantly improving, aircraft since 1928. Harold had established his bold reputation early on, in January 1930, when he and his mentor, Joe Crosson, overcame impossible odds and weeks of extreme weather to locate the crash

Pima Air and Space Museum NC 14260, Tucson, AZ.
*A Lockheed Electra Cockpit.*

site of pilot Carl Ben Eielson and his mechanic, Earl Borland, in northern Siberia. Flying through fog and freezing temperatures in his open cockpit Stearman, Gillam was the least experienced of the pilots involved in the search. He and Crosson were soon given credit for making it possible to recover the bodies of those two greatly admired aviators. He was respected for his courage and uncanny ability to navigate over tough terrain. Old-timers described Alaska weather as *Pan Am weather, normal weather*, or *Gillam weather*—when, often, nobody else wanted to fly. A friend once explained, "We figured God had his hands

Alaska Digital Archives
*Charles Harold Gillam.*

full taking care of Harold!" But, Gillam would simply say, "The weather's never as bad as it looks."

Gillam had experienced his share of heart-stopping takeoffs, near-miss landings, minor accidents, and a few serious crashes. In 1931 alone, Harold miraculously walked away from half a dozen crashes. For his daring and luck, he had been given the popular nickname "Thrill 'em, spill 'em, but no kill 'em Gillam." He hadn't earned that title by playing cards or waiting for the weather to clear and he had never lost a passenger.

Morrison-Knudsen Em Kayan Publication

*"Thrill 'em, spill 'em, but no kill 'em Gillam," Morrison-Knudsen chief pilot.*

We were at war, so another critical factor of travel on the west coast, particularly to or from Alaska, was the great concern about the Japanese. During 1942, there had been a number of submarine-launched torpedoes aimed at coastal sites and at ships. One freighter was hit just outside Los Angeles harbor. Shells had been fired at a Santa Barbara refinery and at a telegraph station on Vancouver Island. Planes launched from submarines had come close to Seattle and the Canadian west coast. One of those planes bombed a national forest in Oregon hoping to cause a holocaust of flame along the coast. Helium-filled barrage balloons had been deployed by the U.S. Army around west coast cities. The military expected that the balloons and their trailing cables would force enemy aircraft to fly at higher altitudes where they would be easier targets for anti-aircraft gunners and their bombing runs would be disrupted.

Post-Intelligencer Collection, Museum of History and Industry

*Barrage balloon, part of Seattle wartime air defenses.*

We were scheduled to depart from Seattle's Boeing Field at ten thirty that Tuesday morning, but were delayed by traffic getting to the airport. Like all travelers going to and from Alaska, we were required to provide official documents authorizing our priority level (usually #5 for civilians and government employees) in order to clear customs and immigration. That was another hurdle that took some time. Then there was a slight mechanical delay as Gillam's attention was called to an oil leak. The line was one to handle an overflow rather than a feed line, so the leak was not considered serious, and it was temporarily mended by use of friction tape and shellac. Packages, then people, were loaded into the airplane. Harold boarded last and latched the door.*

*Observations of George C. Clayton

The Museum of Flight

*Boeing Field, Seattle, Washington … the point of Departure, January 5, 1943.*

A tug pulled the Electra out of the hangar and we took off at 1:30 p.m. Visibility was pretty good, and as we climbed over Seattle we watched the downtown office buildings seem to shrink in size. My fellow passengers that day were Robert Gebo, Morrison-Knudsen's Alaska general contractor; Miss Susan Batzer, traveling to Alaska to take a stenographer job with the CAA; Percy Cutting, a Morrison-Knudsen mechanic; and Dewey Metzdorf, the owner of the Anchorage Hotel and apartments. Dewey was also superintendent of Alaska Railroad's stores, commissary, and hotels. Robert's wife and young son

Anchorage Museum of History and Art

*Hotel Anchorage, owned by passenger Dewey Metzdorf.*

had been at the airfield to see us off. I had previously known Harold Gillam, Percy Cutting, and Bob Gebo, and being rather friendly by nature, I soon became acquainted with the other two. Susan Batzer was greatly thrilled and excited at the prospect of flying to the North. She realized it was an adventure of the first order and that flying over such beautiful, yet treacherous, country was something that few have the privilege of doing.

Robert Gebo, Jr.

*Betty Gebo and son, Robert.*

Our first planned stop was to be on Annette Island, eighteen miles southwest of Ketchikan and about 670 miles from Seattle. It was the most common fueling and rest stop for flights going into and out of Alaska. Our next leg to Anchorage, for example, is another 780 miles to the Northwest. During World War II, the airfield on Annette was home to Royal Canadian Air Force units, including the RCAF 115th fighter squadron and, at various times, to groups of U.S. Army, Navy, and Coast Guard aircraft and personnel. I had been involved with installing some of the communication equipment on the island.

We proceeded to the north with relatively clear skies, passing over Victoria, B.C. about thirty minutes out at 3,000 feet, continuing on a course up the east side of Vancouver Island. As we climbed to 9,000 feet, Robert Gebo, who was sitting in the right front seat and acting as copilot, came back into the cabin and distributed lunch to the rest of the passengers: turkey and cheese sandwiches, grapes, and apples. Numerous times during the eventful trip, I walked up and sat to the side of Susan to visit and point out the highlights of the country we were passing over. Visibility was fine as we passed over Alert Bay, but about 5 p.m. we went into the soup with heavy clouds and increasing turbulence. The aircraft's wings began to accumulate ice. Aware that we were in a war zone, Gillam had maintained radio silence and, flying in the clouds, he became increasingly less sure about his distance and direction toward Annette Island. The airfield also routinely changed its instrument beam to confuse the Japanese and Gillam did not have the correct bearing. We knew we were thirty to forty miles out, but we thought we were farther west than was actually the case. Harold Gillam's reputation of not being intimidated by weather was being tested.

Chip Porter – 2007

*"Expect trouble." Crash Mountain.*

Suddenly, the left engine lost power, sputtered, and quit. With the ice and only one engine, we started losing altitude quite fast, perhaps 3,000 or 4,000 feet in just a couple of minutes. Gillam quickly picked up the microphone and called Ketchikan. "One engine has conked out, expect trouble." Glimpsing mountains through the window, he dropped the mike. He had given no indication of our position. In rough weather and continuing to lose altitude, it was not a question of avoiding a crash; it was now a question of how and where. For twenty lifelong minutes, the plane skimmed treetops with snow-capped peaks occasionally visible through the overcast.

Painting by David Draper

Chapter Two

# SURVIVING THE CRASH

*"A feeling of panic seized me for the moment as*
*I thought I was perhaps the only one alive."*

While waiting for the crash to come, I calmly put on my galoshes. Others did likewise or performed some inconsequential act. There was almost complete silence in the group, each member of the party mentally preparing himself for the end. It was about 6:30 p.m. I yelled at Dewey to fasten his seat belt! Avoiding one mountain, Gillam veered the plane left, then seeing another mountain straight ahead, Harold tried to pancake into an open spot, but the right wing hit two or three trees, shearing off their tops and perhaps slowing us just a little as the wing broke off. Just before impact, to reduce the risk of fire, Gillam cut the power to the still functioning right engine. The crash was as if we were in an explosion—a shuddering impact, the sound of crushing metal, blindness, and pain all at the same moment.

I could feel everything leaving my body and I blacked out. As I came to, I found that my shoulders and head were out of the plane and I had a gash across my forehead. I was standing on my seat through a break in the fuselage. The drizzling rain probably woke me. I called out to the others, but there was no answer. All I could hear was the hissing of the hot engine in the snow. In the darkness, a feeling of panic seized me for the moment as I thought I was perhaps the only one alive. However, I soon heard a response from Gillam who, like me, had sustained a head injury. Others also began to stir. We heard their moans. They were each somewhat pinned in—Gebo against the instrument panel in the copilot's chair, and Cutting and Metzdorf wedged in their seats by the auxiliary gas tank. Fearing fire, the pilot and I started trying to get everyone out of the airplane. Getting Robert Gebo and Dewey Metzdorf free, we pushed them out through the hole in the fuselage. When we went out to look for them, we found they had rolled a distance down behind the aircraft. Percy Cutting had considerable pain in his back. Metzdorf's collarbone was broken

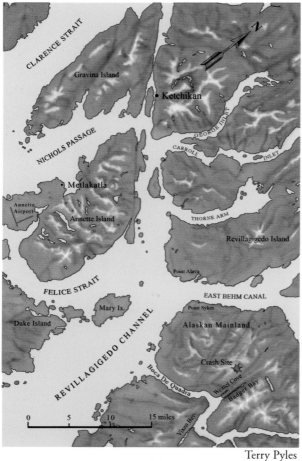

Terry Pyles

*Annette Airport, Ketchikan and Crash Site.*

and Gebo, when he tried to stand, collapsed from a broken leg and fell back into unconsciousness. But the most seriously injured, and pinned in the wreckage, was Susan Batzer. Cutting, Gillam, and I worked two hours to free her, but her arm was nearly severed at the wrist and she was losing substantial amounts of blood. We applied a tourniquet, but she was extremely weak. Her legs were broken and her skull was fractured. We bound up her wounds and gave first-aid treatment as best we could. A steady rain was causing water to leak inside the cabin. Gillam and I lifted a piece of wing cover over the top to shield Susan from the elements. Cutting had seemed okay but, after a little while, he collapsed. His legs were partially paralyzed from his back injury and he pretty much lay flat in the plane for the first three days.

Hall Anderson – 2006

*Crash site is just below a white area, center of picture.*

We had crashed at the top of a ravine, burying the nose of the airplane in twelve feet of snow, and the left wing wedged against the mountain. As a final blow, the top of one tree that had been severed fell across the fuselage. We were about 200 feet below the top of the mountain at an elevation of approximately 1,700 feet above sea level. That may not sound very high, but the mountain was steep, as we were not

33

## Robert Gebo, Seattle, Five Others Aboard Missing Plane

Robert Gebo, Seattle construction engineer and graduate of the University of Washington, and five other persons are missing in an Alaska-bound plane, which took off from Seattle last Tuesday.

A widespread aerial search was being conducted. The plane, piloted by the veteran Alaskan pilot, Harold Gillam, has been unreported since its departure.

On the plane as passenger was 23-year-old Susan Batzer who* joined the Alaska Projects of the Civil Aeronautics Administration in Seattle within the past fortnight.

Gebo, 36 years old, is general superintendent of the Morrison-Knudson Construction Company. His home is at 1964 22nd Ave. W.

**Metzdorf Aboard**

Other passengers were Dewey M. Metzdorf, superintendent of hotels and commissary for the Alaska** Railroad, and who owns the Anchorage Hotel and is an Anchorage civic leader; Joseph H. Tippits, Civil Aeronautics Authority mechanical maintenance-unit employe at Anchorage, and Percy Cutting of Hayward, Calif., a Morrison-Knudson Construction Company employe in Alaska, who was returning from a holiday vacation trip in California.

Officials of both the Morrison-Knudsen Company, which operated the missing plane, and of the Civil Aeronautics Authority said they had high hopes that the missing plane will be found.

Gillam, chief pilot of the company, has been flying in the North for many years and has had many escapes from death.

**'Thrill 'Em, No Kill 'Em'**

C. R. Shinn of Seattle, Alaska manager of the Morrison-Knudsen Company, who went to Anchorage last week, told the Associated Press in Alaska that the plane was stocked with camping equipment and emergency rations.

"Up North, Gillam is known as 'thrill-'em, spill-'em, no kill-'em Gillam'," a C. A. A. official said today. "If anyone can bring his passenger out to safety, it would be he."

Shinn, at Anchorage, said that Canadians report having seen a plane, resembling the missing craft, flying east and later west over the southern part of Vancouver Island. Royal Canadian Air Force bases on the British Columbia coast have joined in the search.

Gebo has worked for the Morrison-Knudson Company for years, and worked on construction for the

**CHARLES H. GILLAM**

*Pilot of lost plane*

company in North Carolina and California before going to Alaska.

Gebo came to the University of Washington from Sheridan, Wyo., after having attended the University of Kansas. He was graduated from the University of Washington in 1930 with the degree of bachelor of science in civil engineering.

Mrs. Robert D. Bedinger, wife of a former Civil Aeronautics Administration official, said that she and her husband had often entertained Gillam in their home and had heard him tell of his many experiences being downed in the North.

"He is the best pilot in Alaska and has been lost many times, and if anyone knows the country and can come out of a difficult spot, he can," said Mrs. Bedinger.

In January, 1930, Gillam attracted international attention when he and Joe Crosson, another Alaskan flyer, found the plane of Carl Ben Eielson and Earl Borland which had been lost on the Siberian coast early in the preceding November on a trip from the ice-bound fur ship, Nanuk.

Miss Batzer lived with an aunt, Mrs. A. W. Olson in Camas, before coming to Seattle. She had attended school in South Dakota and in Portland, Or.

Tippits' home was in Anchorage, where he has lived the past three years.

**January 8, 1943, *The Seattle Times***

*Susan Batzer was actually 25 years old (the newspapers were in error).

**Joseph Tippets had been promoted from Radio Electrician to a position as an "Airways Engineer."

too far from an inlet off the Gulf of Alaska. But at this point, we didn't know where we were at all. For many days, we thought we were on Annette Island.*

In my career with the Civil Aeronautics Administration, I have been present at the scene of many airplane crashes. I can honestly say that I have never seen a plane in the condition ours was in and known anyone to survive. Hitting the trees first likely saved us from instant death. Where I had been sitting, an aluminum window frame dislodged by the impact had been driven directly past with such speed that it became embedded in the side wall of the airplane. Had it hit me, I might have been killed instantly.

That first night we were pretty much down in the ravine under the

Note: They were actually about thirty miles east of the Annette airfield.

tail of the airplane, those of us who could stand holding a tarpaulin over the group. The next day we cleared out an enclosure under the left wing and, with much effort, were able to carry or drag Dewey Metzdorf and Bob Gebo up and place them there with some blankets from the plane. I then spent much of the first two days inside the plane attending to Miss Batzer and Percy Cutting. Susan never complained other than with a little humor asking why I was ripping up *her* slips and pretty things from her luggage to make bandages. I explained hers were the cleanest and nicest we had and then tore another one. She must have sensed she would not live long, but she was conscious and she tried to be cheerful.

Susan had been born in South Dakota. After high school, she attended business college in Portland, Oregon, then moved to Camas, Washington, living with an aunt and uncle and working for Crown-Willamette Paper Company. She had three sisters and her parents now lived in Idaho Falls, which is not far from my birthplace. We talked about Idaho and, although she was not a Latter-day Saint, she knew about the Church and that provided opportunity for additional conversation. During Wednesday night, she spoke frequently of cold feet. The hot water bottle she

William and Blanche Batzer Caughlin
*Susan Batzer, a brave young woman.*

had in her baggage was used to little or no avail. So during the night, I sat on a seat cushion with my bare feet on hers. Unfortunately, we did not have sedatives or drugs to ease her suffering. Percy Cutting was with her when she passed away at about 6:30 p.m. on January 7, almost exactly two days after the crash. She was gracious and sweet, and her courage in the face of death was an inspiration. Just twenty-five years old, she had been as brave as any soldier might have been. We placed her body in the tail end of the airplane and covered it over. It was the best we could do under the circumstances.

Scooping out the snow, and with a bed of pine boughs, we improved the space under the left wing as much as possible. On the sides, we built snow walls and with the pine boughs and some seat cushions from the airplane, we had some comfort. The space was about four or five feet high with room for all four to lie down. We used the engine covers and wing covers to close off the front. We had also opened the nose of the airplane and secured the luggage, two sleeping bags, and five blankets. With constant rain and snow for the first four days, we were pretty unsuccessful in building any fires. After a day or two, we were soaking wet and we discarded what we had on for a change of clothes. When we did start a fire, I put my shoes too close and burned them. From then on, I was entirely without shoes. I merely wrapped my feet in rags.

In the long days that followed, we learned a little about each other's lives. Percy Cutting, who preferred being called "Sandy," had grown up in the northern woods of New England and New Brunswick, Canada, but now lived in Hayward, California. He had been there with his wife, Ruby, and four children for Christmas. Harold Gillam's wife, Nell, was at their home in Fairbanks, but their three children* (a boy and two girls) were living with Harold's mother in Seattle. He had been with his kids over the holidays. Robert (Bob) Gebo had been raised in Sheridan, Wyoming. He had been very athletic and, in fact, he played freshman football at the University of Kansas. He subsequently transferred to the University of Washington where he graduated with a civil engineering degree. He also met his wife, Elizabeth (Betty), there at the University of Washington. Bob and Betty had one son, Robert, Jr., who was about five months younger than my son, John. Betty and Robert, Jr. were also in the Seattle area. Alaska authorities had strongly suggested that the place for women and children was in the states. Throughout the 1930s,

*Harold Gillam's first son by a previous marriage, Harold, Jr., lived with his mother.

Bob Gebo had worked as an engineer and supervisor on several major construction projects across the lower 48. Dewey Metzdorf's family was in Seattle, where his two boys attended a boarding school. His wife and boys had previously lived in Alaska, but with the war concerns, they were spending the school year in Seattle. Dewey lived in Anchorage in his hotel and Bob Gebo, when he was in Anchorage, also stayed at the hotel. In fact, the Anchorage Hotel was effectively the headquarters for Morrison-Knudsen's Alaska operations.

Robert Gebo, Jr.

*Robert Gebo (on the left) at his Anchorage Hotel office.*

When we crashed, they all knew I was the LDS branch president in Anchorage and that I was proud of this, and when I suggested that we have prayer every day as a group, they were all very anxious to do so. However, after four or five days, one of the men (Cutting) felt any further mention of families and such things as prayer reminded us of our plight and was too depressing and he asked that we not pray vocally anymore. We all followed his request, but I'm sure that these men, like me, never quit praying. As a matter of fact, I got to where I had a regular trail from the wreck to some rocks where I went to pray, making a pretty good practice of it. And, not only did I feel I should, but I knew it would be helpful.

One of the things I prayed for most was that my family would know that I had survived the crash and would hold on until being rescued. I later learned that my wife and my seven sisters never doubted for a minute that I was alive. I am sure our prayers gave us confidence and helped sustain the good relationships that prevailed among us for the entire time.

In addition to my scriptures, one book I had with me was *Unto the Hills* by Richard L. Evans. Evans was the host of the popular Mormon Tabernacle Choir radio program from Temple Square in Salt Lake City. His weekly commentaries on the radio, called the "Spoken Word," were combinations of lofty thoughts and simple wisdom. *Unto the Hills* was a collection of those sermonettes and over the days we spent camped under the wing of the airplane, I read them to the group. We read the whole book. The philosophies of the different chapters gave us much to talk about and those conversations were a way to pass the time and to keep our minds in a proper state. Several of the sermonettes spoke, in a manner, to our current predicament, our dependence on each other, our hopes for rescue and our prayers for our Heavenly Father's protection and guidance. Thinking about the Tabernacle Choir during our difficult circumstances, I often recalled the pioneer song, "Come, Come, Ye Saints," its lyrics calling for determination and courage despite any adversity. The 23rd Psalm was also a comfort.

As was pretty standard practice for any aircraft flying in Alaska in those days, there were emergency food provisions on the plane: two pounds of dried beans, four cans of corned beef, five cans of sardines, fourteen bars of chocolate, two pounds of hardtack, eight boxes of bouillon cubes, a pound of coffee, and a pound of tea. We also had six bottles of ABC vitamin pills which Adeline, Dewey Metzdorf's wife, had sent with him. By being frugal, we thought we could make the food last for several weeks.[2] Thankfully, we also had a box of matches. On the second day, we each had two cups of bouillon and split a candy bar among us. On the third day we cooked some beans, but without seasoning of any kind, they were not very appealing.

[2] F.A. Zeusler, *Sea Drift*, Air-Sea Rescue in Alaska.

As we stretched our food supply, our whole day's rations were generally not more than a cup of bouillon, which we made by melting snow and dropping a bouillon cube into it, and perhaps a few raisins or a piece of sardine. We would take a sardine and cut it into

USCG – 1943

*Mountains near Boca de Quadra.**
*(Now part of Misty Fjords National Monument Wilderness.)*

four pieces and this small portion was our food for the day. We realized we must keep something in our stomachs. It's a funny thing, too, how those candy bars became a very important staple. When you really begin to lose your energy, a bite of chocolate, those little squares, seemed to really be a boost, so that became the most precious of our commodities. We broke them up, counted and sorted them. We each

* "Mouth of Quadra." A deep, fifty-mile long inlet named for the Spanish explorer of the Pacific Northwest, Don Juan Francisco de la Bodega Y Quadra, born in Lima, Peru in 1743.

had one square a day at any time of the day we wanted, but that was it. But, of course, this was far short of the nourishment we really needed. At some point, Dewey Metzdorf remarked, "Everything I eat tastes like pine needles."

The snow was deep, but the weather was alternating rain and snow so it was very soft. Working my way about on the third or fourth day, I plunged through the surface and sank clear up to my neck. On Saturday, the fourth day, it did clear up, but it was extremely cold. Early on the fifth day, with the snow stopped, the wind sprang up and blew for awhile with such force that we couldn't stand up against it.

Cutting was able to create our first real signal fire, doing so in a hollow tree. But we knew we would not be easy to see. On the third day, three planes (likely RCAF) which we heard and then saw to the south were obviously searching for us. We shot off magnesium flares and shouted, but we were not seen or heard. The next day, an Alaska Game Commission plane circled a ridge opposite where we were several times. He flew so close, but below us, that we could even make out the pilot. Through the valley below he was heading for the coast, apparently assuming that, in trouble, we would have tried to get down to a beach to land and look for rescue. It was a good assumption but, of course, we hadn't made it to the beach. We were disappointed, but it was at least encouraging that they were looking for us.

Chip Porter – 2007

*Crash site view toward Badger Lake.*

Chapter Three
# STARVING AND FREEZING

*"He was truly risking his life in trying to help
all of us have an opportunity to survive."*

During the fifth day, there was a somewhat encouraging sound: an explosion which both the pilot and I recognized was likely from the rock quarry on Annette Island. Harold and Sandy went up the ridge to try to get oriented and to confirm to a degree where we might be. What we didn't realize was how far in that cool air and wilderness silence the sound was carried from the quarry. It seemed much closer than it really was and, looking at our maps, we determined where we might possibly be on Annette. We were confused and wrong. Annette and the quarry were about thirty miles to the west.

Coming back, Harold selected a modest amount of provisions and supplies, including matches, a parachute, and some magnesium flares from the plane. He then set out to find his way toward the sound of the explosions. He was no stranger to survival in the Alaska wilderness and based on his past experience, he fully expected to find someone or be discovered and be able to bring rescue to the rest of us. We never heard from him again. We have no idea what pain and anguish he may have experienced. He was truly risking his life in trying to help all of us survive.

CAA

*Rock Quarry on Annette Island, "We didn't realize how far the sound carried."*

Harold Gillam left on Sunday, January 10. For the next several days, the remaining four of us settled ourselves in, hoping for his success, but also carefully rationing our very limited food, realizing he might not survive. Our major activities were just collecting wood and keeping up the fire. We heard planes a couple more times. We also were realizing that soon we must get down off the mountain. We were hungry and cold and it was agony to attempt to move around. Our bones might have been healing, but we were gradually not only starving, but also suffering from exposure. The temperature felt like it was well below zero. Gangrene was now a risk to all of us, but Dewey

Metzdorf and Bob Gebo were in particularly bad shape. Bob, for example, had been wearing everyday dress shoes. Gradually he lost feeling in his toes, his feet turning white, then black. Besides all this, we also realized that the search for us was likely to be abandoned soon.

I remember going into the plane one afternoon to search for leftovers from the lunch we had eaten just before the crash. It all came back clearly. I got down on the floor of the plane and went through it bit by bit, picking up crumbs of bread, frozen grapes, and disintegrated apples. I put them all on something and took this little tray back up under the wing where we were living. Given our circumstances, these little pieces of food were really a treat at the time. I thought for a while that frozen grapes must be the greatest thing since home cooking. We didn't have many, but they sweetened our mouths and renewed our spirits just a little.

About the fifteenth, I realized it was my son's second birthday and oh, how I wished I was there! The pain of separation from my family was severe. I prayed for Johnny and his new brother or sister that they would know of my love for them and my hopes and dreams for their future. These thoughts only strengthened my resolve to stay alive.

Sandy Cutting went to the top of the mountain and could see where Gillam had gone down on the other side. He could also see a bay in the opposite direction in the distance to the north. (We later learned this was Smeaton Bay.) The next day, Cutting took a sleeping bag, a little food, and the .22 caliber rifle which was part of the aircraft's emergency equipment. He went down the mountain to the north and, reaching the water at Smeaton Bay on Sunday, built a signal fire and kept it burning on Sunday and Monday. He found the beach rocky and the shore strewn with slabs of ice. There was no sign of life. He felt this bay was not part of any regular shipping route and rescue there would be unlikely. Starting back, he suddenly got lucky and shot five grouse, one of which he cooked and ate for energy.

Describing his return, Sandy said, "I had a long climb ahead of me to reach our camp.… As I started out, I was so whipped, it was an effort to get to my feet. Then it seemed to get even tougher. As I climbed,

I stumbled up, hanging on to a tree for support. Finally, I was so tired that I crawled on my hands and knees into the camp… With my four hens, I received a hero's welcome. Four days alone had made my voice so hoarse that I could hardly speak. Thank heavens, though, I hadn't reached the point where I talked and answered myself."[3]

Chip Porter - 2007

*Sandy Cutting went North to a body of water we later learned was Smeaton Bay.*

On the next day, January 20, we boiled two of the grouse, ate the meat, and drank the broth. There's not much to a spruce hen but the breast, but what there was, was good eats. They saved our lives!

For a day or so, Cutting rested to recover from his strenuous hike down to the water and then back up to the plane. We realized now that staying on that mountain was no longer a viable plan as we were just gradually freezing and starving to death, so we started preparing for all of us to move our camp down to the valley floor. We were mak-

[3] "Hell in God's Country," *Alaska Life*, August 1943

ing the move actually for three reasons: (1) thinking there might be a greater chance of being sighted by planes going through the valley (if the search had not been abandoned); (2) hoping the cold might

be less severe, and (3) possibly shooting a deer or other game. We had seen one Sitka blacktail deer at a great distance earlier. By Friday, January 22 (day 17), we were ready to make the descent. Clothing, five blankets, two sleeping bags, cooking utensils, the axe, hunting knife, gun and ammunition, two containers of gasoline, and the blow torch were all bundled into the tarpaulins that had covered the wing and motor. Dewey Metzdorf

Andrew Piston
*Southeast Alaska Blue Grouse.*

was able to rescue from his suitcase a small ceramic dachshund that his youngest son, Dewey Jr., had given him for Christmas.

The going was miserable. We were sliding and crawling, and Robert Gebo had limited mobility, walking and sort of dragging his slowly mending leg. Metzdorf was perhaps even more in pain with a broken collarbone and broken ribs. It was, in places, an almost vertical drop and there was no form of trail. We had to deal with ice and heavy snow drifts and were constantly climbing over fallen logs, rocks, and low brush. We couldn't carry our packs, but just stumbled along dragging them behind us. For about half the way down, we were able to use one of the airplane's doors sort of as a sled. We were dragging and lowering part of our supplies, wet clothing, and so forth, then going back over the same few feet with the next portion.

We were weak and frostbitten, and the trip was so difficult and painful that it almost broke us.

About two-thirds down the mountain, we got out of the deep snow and that night made camp on a ledge which jutted out just enough to give us room for a fire and a place to lay the two sleeping bags. We had saved the last two of the spruce hens to give us a little extra nourishment for the journey. We cooked and ate them that Friday night. We took turns, with two of us trying to sleep while the other two stoked the fire, but it was a terrible night with constant rain and sleet and, even with a fire, we were unable to get warm. We had, by this time, each grown large, disreputable-looking beards and had sort of weird vacant looks in our eyes. It wasn't good. I'd hate to have crossed our paths on a dark night!

←Crash

USCG – 1943

*Base camp* ↑

The next day, Saturday, we made it to the valley floor and searched out a place to make a new camp on the edge of a forest and an open area. As we approached where we would actually set up camp, Cutting did shoot a little red squirrel. We boiled him and savored that pretty tasteless soup. In fact, we may have sipped that squirrel broth for about five "meals." When you're that hungry, it's not the actual nourishment, it's what you think it is. The psychologists might say it is mind over matter, but he was a welcome replenishment to our now all but expended larder.

There had been one apparent miracle in our struggle down the mountain. A piece that had been broken in Gebo's leg bone had somehow become wedged back into place and had remained set.

With tree boughs, twigs, and using the motor covers, we were able to make a fairly comfortable camp just into the timber. Cutting had spent much of his youth in the woods and those experiences and skills were enormously helpful. While he did much of the building of the camp, I made trips back up to our trail to move the remainder of our bundles down. On Monday, January 25, I set about using the axe and building up a stock of firewood while Sandy took the .22 to hunt. He was unsuccessful. The snow was too deep, and any game which might have been there in another season had moved on to warmer areas. That afternoon, there was another terrible snowstorm, which was very discouraging. I went out in the trees in back of our camp and prayed. I had prayed so much that it had really got beyond the business of prayer. It seemed to be a matter of talking to God and having an understanding with him of our needs. I wanted to know what we should do and when we should do it. And I prayed again that my wife would know that I was alive.

*Alta and Johnny at home in Anchorage.*

Chapter Four
# WHAT ABOUT ALTA?

*"She (Alta) has either totally lost it and is living
in a dream world or she really has had a revelation and
knows something that none other can comprehend."*

Some weeks later, I learned how difficult it was for Alta as she followed the news and anxiously waited for more definite word about our fate.

The radio message from Harold Gillam hadn't been much help to potential rescuers, neither was the harshness of the weather or the terrain of the region where it was thought we were lost. Based on flying time and the average speed of the aircraft, it had been assumed that we had gotten within 60 miles of Annette Island.

Coast Guard Subsection Commander Frederick A. Zeusler took charge, but he would have significant support from the Canadians on Annette Island and out of Prince Rupert. Grids were laid out and small grid squares were assigned for intensive searches, with priority given to possible and probable designations. Most hopes were that Gillam had accomplished a beach landing, a relatively common practice of bush pilots when their planes were in distress. Water areas were covered by planes and by boats, shorelines by boat and on foot; the land and mountains by planes and shore patrols. The rescue team consisted of six American and two Canadian vessels as well as two Canadian and five American airplanes. One of the American planes was a Fairchild from the Alaska Wildlife Service piloted by Ray Renshaw. Personnel involved in the search included the Ketchikan coast guard servicemen (trained by Chief Boatswain Arthur Hook, USCGR), aided by the Territorial Guard, a group of local hunters and fishermen as well as some forestry men, miners, cannery workers, and Indians who knew the country well and how to live in it.

Alaska's Digital Archives
*U.S. Coast Guard vessels out of Ketchikan were involved in the search.*

Because a plane heard over British Columbia at about 4:30 p.m. was thought to have been our aircraft, the southern portion of the search included a wide area, hundreds of miles of wilderness from the interior of British Columbia to the shorelines and islands of the Inside Passage. By the eighth day, the Morrison-Knudsen Company joined the search, sending veteran pilot Don Brady and two others, Thomas Donohoe and Harry Bowman, to Ketchikan in an M-K plane. The men were close friends of Harold and expressed their desire to leave no stone unturned to find us. A few days later, another M-K plane flown by Gillam Air Services pilot, Frank Barr, accompanied by his mechanic, headed to Whitehorse to begin searching the Upper Skeena River Valley. But all the efforts undertaken by the Royal Canadian Air Force, the U.S. Navy, Coast Guard, and others were unsuccessful.

USCG

*The Mighty Mac, the USCGC McLane.*

One of the coast guard vessels assigned to the search was the *McLane*, operating under the direction of the navy. The sea search was in conjunction with regular patrol duties within a sixty-mile radius of Annette Island. The first search by ship covered the inland waters and Dixon Entrance. Smaller craft were directed to search the shoreline, commencing with Hidden Inlet and as far north as Ketchikan shores, Mary Island, Annette Island, Duke Island, Bold Island, and both shores of Clarence Strait. Another vessel involved in the search was a 46-foot buoy tender, the *Tucsan*. It had been a fishing boat commissioned for wartime service with the Coast Guard Reserve.

After the first week, the headlines in the *Anchorage Daily Times*, Tuesday, January 12, read "Gillam Search Still Snagged, Hope Dims." "Planes Must Await Better Flight Weather" and "Officials Admit Situation Looks like Disaster after Week of Silence." The newspaper described the weather conditions as having prevented searches the previous day (Monday), as it had over the weekend. Unfavorable features of the situation seemed to be piling up as day after day passed without any new developments. But one article contained significant insights and, in some ways, was also a premonition about our circumstances:

> … the possibility that the airplane crashed into a mountain at a high altitude. While such a crash may not have taken the lives of the passengers, the odds are against their being unharmed by the experience.
>
> However, in such an event it was felt that some member of the party should make an appearance somewhere after mushing out from the wilderness… . Officials conceded that the party might be encamped near the wrecked plane awaiting assistance… .
>
> Many instances are known in Alaskan aviation where parties have been lost for long periods and have turned up safe and unharmed. Confidence has been expressed continually if the party landed safely, the members will provide amply for themselves.… In addition to the experienced bush pilot, at least two of the five passengers, Dewey Metzdorf and Joseph H. Tippets, have had experience on the trail in Alaska.[4]

A few days after the accident, Ruby Cutting, in talking to a *Hayward Review* reporter, had expressed a similar confidence about Percy. "If the plane has been forced down, I know he will come out all right. He is strong and resourceful and an excellent woodsman."

[4]Anchorage Daily Times, Jan. 12, 1943.

That same week, there was a temporary diversion when a plane piloted by Gren Collins went missing for twenty-four hours. Ray Petersen, of Petersen Air Service, and Gordon McKenzie, of Alaska Star Airlines, flew two planes back and forth between Anchorage and Fairbanks without finding them. The next day, Frank Barr, in his Stinson tri-motor spotted Collins and his mechanic, Lawrence Barr, next to a lake where they had been forced down by engine trouble. It was a bit of good news that everyone welcomed.

Gradually, however, the stories that Alta saw in the *Anchorage Daily Times* became shorter and reflected more frustration and disappointment as no signs of us had been found. After January 19, the Anchorage newspaper made little mention of the crash. Roy Clift, a CAA colleague, in a note to my sister, Mary Mahoney, wrote "… terribly sorry I can't give you better news than this," to which he attached an article from the Seattle, Washington newspaper:

### Army Halts Search for Missing Plane

Abandonment by American and Canadian Air Force planes of the three-week search for missing Morrison-Knudsen company airplane with six aboard was reported here today.

The plane, with pilot Harold Gillam at the controls, vanished after leaving Seattle January 5 on a flight to Alaska. An unceasing search has been maintained from the air along the wild British Columbia coast without discovery of any definite clue to the Lockheed Electra's fate.

Two company planes have pressed the search steadily whenever weather permitted, but it is not known whether they would continue their fruitless hunt, in view of the withdrawal of military planes.

Dewey Metzdorf, Jr., had been calling his mother every day from his boarding school, hoping to learn some news about his father, but after the search was abandoned, he sadly discontinued those calls, presuming all hope was lost.

The president of the Northwestern States Mission of the LDS Church, Desla Bennion, wrote to Alta on January 22 to express his sympathy:

> The information I just received over the telephone long distance from Mr. Snow of the Morrison-Knudsen Company of Seattle, telling of the final abandonment of the search for your husband and the other members of the missing plane is heartrending.
>
> It is hard for us to understand, Sister Tippets, why a man so worthy and with such a high purpose in life should be called. We just have to rest ourselves with faith in the Lord and with a knowledge and assurance that your husband lived his life the best he could, and died in the service of the Lord and his country, and that you will meet him again in another world and carry on with him throughout eternity.
>
> I take it that in the not-too-distant future you may be coming this way, and can assure you that when you do we would like to meet you and have you stay with us. You will need to rest yourself on your long journey. If you could let us know, we will meet you in Seattle, or wherever it is possible for us to make contact with you. Sister Bennion joins me in expressing our deepest sympathy, and rest assured that our prayers are ever with you for your own safekeeping, as well as that of your son.
>
> Praying our Heavenly Father to help you and to give you strength and courage to carry on...

President Bennion, on January 22, also wrote a letter to the First Presidency of the Church to report on my seeming death. "President Tippets has done an outstanding work all over Alaska, as the CAA called him into various locations. He accomplished a great mission in the organization of our people and, particularly in his case, of men in uniform.... His death is a great loss to the people of Alaska, as well as to the Church." Acting on that letter, the First Presidency of the Church then wrote directly to Alta in a letter dated January 26.

CHURCH OF JESUS CHRIST OF LATTER DAY SAINTS
OFFICE OF THE FIRST PRESIDENCY
SALT LAKE CITY, UTAH

HEBER J. GRANT, PRESIDENT
J. REUBEN CLARK, JR, FIRST COUNSELOR
DAVID O. McKAY, SECOND COUNSELOR

January 26, 1943

Mrs. Alta Elizabeth Tippets
Box 2127
Anchorage, Alaska

Dear Sister Tippets:

It is with deep sorrow that we received today notice that
search for the missing plane and its occupants on which your husband
was flying, has been given up.

We have not been favored with an acquaintance with yourself,
but we had the blessing of knowing your husband and of appreciating
at least in part his loyalty to the work of the Lord, his devotion,
and the righteousness of his life. Presidents Clark and McKay had
the pleasure of visiting with him when he was in Salt Lake City. They
both speak in the highest terms of him.

We know we can say nothing that will compensate much for your
great loss, a loss which is shared with you by the saints of Anchorage
and vicinity, and through them by the whole Church. We can only yield
to the ancient wisdom of Job: "The Lord gave, and the Lord hath taken
away; blessed be the name of the Lord."

We may not know the purposes of the Lord in bringing back to
Him strong, valiant souls tabernacled in the flesh; but we can see
that the passing to the other side of hundreds of thousands—unfortunately
including very many of our own brethren—under the conditions in which
most of them now go, with war hate in their hearts, raises problems on
the other side which might be aided by the spirits of men of strong
faith and righteous lives here on the earth, such as was your husband.

May the Lord bless you and give you peace and comfort in your
great bereavement is our humble prayer.

Faithfully your brethren,

*[signatures]*

The First Presidency

Alta's faith and hope for our survival remained extremely firm, but "what to do with Alta," my dear wife, was getting lots of attention.

One day, Mac McCarrey asked me to talk to her and tell her she had to face reality, that Joe was dead and she needed to make some decisions about her life and Johnny and David (the planned name for the expected baby if it was a boy). She convinced me he was okay. She had complete faith. Nothing could shake it.

*Mildred Hackett*

Sadly, not long after this, Alta suffered the loss of the new baby she was carrying. It was a great disappointment and only added to the emotional and physical strain she was already going through.

During this same time, a more hopeful letter was sent by Nicholas G. Smith, an assistant to the Twelve Apostles of the Church. Brother Smith had known my Tippets family from Farmington, Utah, and knew Alta and me because he had been the Northwestern States Mission president when the Anchorage Branch was organized. In his letter, written to the Anchorage Branch leaders, Elder Smith was responding to a "What should we do about Alta?" question. His answer, in part, was that they should trust her judgment to allow for the possibility that she truly had a knowledge given of God that I was alive and would yet be found.

As of Tuesday, January 26, after we had been lost for twenty-one days, the search was discontinued. Almost all concerned except my wife, Alta, had finally given up hope of finding us alive. The United States and Canadian governments said there was no chance, but Alta stuck to her belief that I had survived.

On that Tuesday… I was sitting in my home reading a book. A couple of the branch members had been visiting me to give me comfort and ease my anxiety. As I was reading, I received a very definite impression that my husband was alive…. that he had started out from his camp that day…. I wished the search would be continued. I told this to the other members of the Anchorage branch presidency and also to the CAA officials who visited with me. I knew my husband was alive because the impression came so strongly. I went to bed that night and had the first restful unbroken sleep I had had in three weeks.

Captain Harold Johnson, who served in the branch with me, and J. L. McCarrey, a lawyer and close friend, came by that day. Cora McCarrey remembered her husband returning to the car after having visited with Alta. He said to his wife that "Alta has either totally lost it and is living in a dream world or she really has had a revelation and knows something that none other can hardly comprehend." Alta's only concession was that, if they would give her one more week, if I was not found, she would at that point follow their advice and start making plans to leave Alaska. Despite everything, she was still confident that I was okay. One of our friends from church, Omer Smith, described how Alta wouldn't believe otherwise, and kept our home and family as if I were just away on an extended trip.

Wilford René Richardson, a young LDS soldier, was another visitor that week. Taking an army 2½-ton truck over to our house, he offered to help Alta move or do anything else for her that she needed. René long recalled her words, "I don't know if you will understand, but I have been praying and this morning I have had positive assurance that Joseph is coming back."

Alta's faith was also helped by remembering stories from childhood of her great-grandparents' trials crossing the plains to Utah in 1856 as part of the ill-fated Willie Handcart Company. Thomas Moulton, with his wife and five children, including two-year-old Sophie, survived cold and hunger as the company was trapped by early snowstorms in the mountains of Wyoming. Sophie was Alta's grandmother.

Chip Porter – 2007

*Weasel Point.*

## Chapter Five
# WEASEL COVE

*"… We were keenly disappointed. Instead of a
sandy beach, we found only rocks and cliffs."*

Although our new camp at the bottom of the mountain was, in some ways, an improvement, death by starvation was still our likely fate. Somehow, someone had to try to get to a point where help might be found. After discussion, it was agreed that Sandy and I should go, and we reluctantly left the other two men on Tuesday, January 26. To give our companions some comfort, we said we would go two days and then, if our search was not productive, we would return. That would allow them to hold out for at least four days with some hope. Dividing the food was easy because there wasn't any. We left what we had with Bob and Dewey—two bouillon cubes and about two teaspoons of tea. We filled containers with water and put everything within close reach for them.

Our thought in starting out for help was that if we could reach the body of water we had seen in the distance to the south, there might be a possibility of walking along the shore until we could reach some sort of habitation. It was a wild hope, but the Lord had given us each a brain and a sound body, and we felt we should give him a chance to lead us out of our predicament.

I took some courage from memories of my own grandfather's difficult experiences in the winter of 1847. John Harvey Tippets had been a member of the "Mormon Battalion" in the war with Mexico, marching to Santa Fe in December 1846. From there, he and Thomas Woolsey were dispatched to accompany a sick detachment north to Pueblo, Colorado. Continuing north and then to the east, the two men took the battalion's mail to their families and church leaders at Winter Quarters, near Omaha, Nebraska. My grandfather, together with Thomas Woolsey, was lost in blizzards, had little food, and was captured by Indians (from whom they soon escaped). Grandfather Tippets and Woolsey reached Winter Quarters in desperate condition, stumbling into camp on February 15, 1847, having traveled for fifty-two days and covering about 750 miles. Our plight there in the Alaska wilderness did not seem to be any worse than theirs had been.

It took us all day trudging through the valley to get to the shore of the bay, as it turned out to be. We didn't walk—we shuffled. I had fashioned the pieces of blanket wrapped around my feet with other materials from the plane to be almost like mukluks.* Cutting's foot gear was a pair of slippers and galoshes. As it was, our feet became frostbitten and in bad shape, as were our hands. We had to stop often to help pull each other out of the eight-foot-deep snow but, gratefully, the muskeg** holes were frozen over. The country was so rough we could hardly make any progress at all. Rocks and logs were hidden under the snow and some stretches were quite steep,

* Eskimo boots of skins and furs.
** Muskeg is the Alaska word for swampy bogs, wet, unstable muck and moss incapable of sustaining much weight.

Chip Porter – 2007

*Valley floor and looking toward Weasel Cove.*

making it necessary to zigzag back and forth. We tried to follow a stream. By cutting holes in the ice, we tried to fish, but there was not a single bite. It seemed that every effort to supply food ended in discouragement. We were traversing some of the worst country I have ever seen. But, Sandy was keeping us out of trouble as he seemed to have an uncanny sense of figuring out the right way to

61

get around an obstacle or to pick a right trail. The total distance from the base camp to the water was about three miles, but it felt to us as many times that.

Chip Porter – 2007

*Rough going.*

Chip Porter – 2007

*We tried to fish, but no luck.*

Nearing the shore that night, we dug a deep hole, scraped the snow off a large tree trunk, and slept on it. We wrapped our arms around each other and huddled together in the single light sleeping bag we had, realizing we must preserve every bit of our precious body heat. There was very little rest. We had to take turns waking each other up to see if the other was still alive. Sometimes we froze together, and it took a tremendous effort to become separated again.

When thoughts came to me that Sandy might die, I was seized with panic. We needed each other. If one should go, the other would surely die, and likewise the other two men we had left behind. Their lives depended on us. This thought helped to sustain us in the almost superhuman task of carrying on.

Chip Porter – 2007

*Reaching Weasel Cove.*

Finally at the shore of the bay (Weasel Cove), we were keenly disappointed. Instead of a sandy beach, we found only rocks and cliffs. We couldn't get down to the water. We waited for a change of tide, but receding waters exposed only more rocks. It was necessary for us to travel in the woods along the side of the bay until we located a place where we could get down to the water. There was not much in the scene to encourage us, with ice floating in the water. It looked cold—and it was!

Chip Porter 2007

*Beach of logs and rocks.*

Moving down along the west side of the cove, we reached a point where we could see the framework of a cabin across the water. We just had to get to that cabin to see if there was food and shelter. There was considerable driftwood and logs along the rocky beach, so we started to build a raft, tearing one of our remaining blankets into strips to tie the logs together. After it was complete, we tried it out. The raft tipped, functioning almost like a teeter-totter. I would go low in the water and stroke, and Sandy went down as I rose up. But we soon started to sink, so I jumped off and Sandy headed for the opposite shore.

Chip Porter – 2007

*"Sandy" Cutting reaches beach near cabin.*

Based on some old newspapers he found inside, Cutting determined the cabin had been abandoned for at least a couple of years, but he discovered an old, leaky boat, and found a small can of tar, a cup of rice with weevils, and some cinnamon and cayenne pepper. With his findings, he started back across the bay, towing the boat behind the raft. However, as he neared the shore where I was waiting, the winds and tide changed. I was absolutely helpless to aid him as he battled the waves to get back to safety. We thought we had experienced every emotion up to that time, but the feeling that gripped me when it looked as if Sandy might never be able to make it back to land is a feeling I never care to experience again. Dependent on each other as we were, the strain of trying to get back together and having the tide separating us farther all the time was almost more than we could stand. He fought for hours before he could get the raft back to where I could wade out and help pull it in.

Sandy and I then made our way stumbling back to where I had kept a campfire burning. Famished, we cooked the rice and weevils; if you think about it as sort of carbohydrates and protein, it was a veritable feast. The next morning, we worked to repair the old boat. We first tried cutting a blanket into strips to plug up the holes, but when we tried to launch it, the boat filled with water and sank. We then tried using kapok from our sleeping bags mixed with the tar Sandy had found in order to plug the holes. This time it worked. In the afternoon, we started back across the cove over to the cabin. As we drew closer to the shore, a seam in our boat opened and we started to sink. We swam the rest of the way pulling the boat behind us.

Chip Porter – 2007

*Cabin remains.*

## Chapter Six
# BOCA DE QUADRA

*"When… I smacked my lips over its delicious
flavor, he agreed to have his half."*

As if in answer to prayer, several crows flew down and lighted on a rock quite near us. Given the beating and having been nearly drowned in salt water, if our .22 rifle would even work was a big question, but it did. Sandy's aim was good, his hand was steady, and he shot three of them forthwith. We immediately set to work to eat them—all but the feathers. We didn't wait long to roast them either, they were just slightly warmed through. There wasn't much to them, but I never knew that anything could be as delicious as roasted crow breast. In our circumstances, they seemed like turkey legs. I told Sandy that the liver was the choicest part to me of fowl meat and he urged me to have all of it. When, however, I smacked my lips over its delicious flavor, he agreed to have his half.

The cabin was near to the point, and from there we could see what appeared to be cannery buildings to the south of us. The next day (day 24), we set out across Boca de Quadra. After hours of laborious paddling, we managed to make it across to the buildings only to find them long deserted and falling to pieces. We had hoped to find some food, but that item was so nonexistent that even the rats had left. We debated whether we should burn the building or the oil tank for a signal. It was quite a temptation, but there was a "Do Not Destroy" sign, so we forgot the whole thing and started back, bailing our boat constantly. The boat kept afloat long enough for us to cross the bay. The round trip took us seven hours. In hindsight, I wished we had at least burned that old oil tank. Someone surely would have seen the blaze and investigated.

Courtesy of Pat Roppel

*Quadra, Alaska Cannery 1935.*

In testing out the boat again, and after making a few more repairs, we became somewhat bold. We were on a point of land jutting out into the bay, which had a narrow outlet to the sea. We felt if we could make our way out to the open water, we would have a chance to get to Annette Island or find some inhabited place where we could get help.

On Saturday (day 25), we started out. We knew our chances were slim, but desperation and concern for our two comrades back in camp forced us to make a try. We sat in the bottom of the boat, actually sitting in the icy cold water. The boat leaked almost as fast as we could bail. We bailed with one hand and paddled wearily with the other for about an hour. There was only one inch of space on the side of the boat above the water. After a couple hundred yards, we had to run the boat to shore and tip it over to empty it, and then start again.

Chip Porter – 2007

*Cannery Site, Boca de Quadra.*

We should not have undertaken that trip. Before we left, I had a clear feeling that we should not go. It was more than a feeling, it was a warning. But we set out and, as a result, we were headed for disaster. In Sandy's words, "We didn't have brains enough to stay put."

After we'd been rowing about two hours, a violent storm began to develop. The sky turned black and the waves got higher and higher, heavy swells forcing us to bail even faster to keep afloat. Nearly full of water, the boat capsized and we were dumped into the bay, chilling to the bone in the bitterly cold water. Cakes of ice were floating all around us. We lost our overcoats, cooking utensils, everything but the clothing we had on and our rifle.

Weasel Cove    Weasel Point              Badger Bay

Chip Porter – 2007

*Boca de Quadra.*

Our clothing dragged us down and the waves tossed us around. Just for a moment, I lost all faith and was angry with the Lord. *Why, I thought, have you let me go through so much, for so long, only to drown here today?* But, almost as I completed that thought, with my head barely above water, I found my feet touching the bottom. Pushing off and trying to swim, we kept together and made it the short distance to the shore. But we found only rocky cliffs. The waves were dashing us against the slippery rocks and then drawing us back into the water. We could not find a hold. Our hands were so cold we could not hold on when we did get a chance. It took us more than a half hour to finally grasp a ledge and pull ourselves fully out of the water. In excruciating pain we climbed what seemed to be sixty feet to the top of the cliff. All we could do was lie there completely exhausted, soaked, and miserable. I think if either of us had been a cigarette smoker we wouldn't have had the strength—the margin was that narrow.

Chip Porter – 2007

*Cliff Area.*

Our hands and feet were bleeding. Our clothes were quickly freezing on us. Normally, a man falling into water at those temperatures would suffer shock and likely drown. Doctors later told us, however, that our long period of exposure to cold had conditioned our bodies to the elements and that shock just didn't happen. Certainly, I thought, the good Lord must be protecting us.

Fortunately, we had kept our matches in a bouillon cube tin sealed with adhesive tape and they were dry. We made a small fire and tried to warm our feet. It was like trying to thaw out a piece of ice. We then set out to try and return to our camp, encouraging each other as we went. Our clothes froze in the angle of a bent leg and all we could do was shuffle our feet. Every little while we had to stop and build a fire to thaw out a little.

After traveling some distance, we saw an object on the shore of the bay. On investigation, we found the remains of our old boat which had been washed up on the shore, beaten against the rocks, and smashed. Under the seat, I found my valuable bundle of documents and papers, still wrapped in oilcloth. Somehow they were still preserved and dry. Included in the bundle were my Bible, Book of Mormon, and the *Unto*

71

*the Hills* book. My scriptures had greatly helped me to keep up my faith and filled me with renewed courage and hope. Recovering them seemed to be a small but special miracle.

Another source of encouragement came from a short poem, "Don't Quit," which at some point I had clipped out and pasted in the little notebook I had been carrying. Under our circumstances, these lines seemed especially appropriate:

## Don't Quit
When things go wrong, as they sometimes will,
When the road you're trudging seems all up hill,

When care is pressing you down a bit,
Rest, if you must—but don't you quit.

Success is failure turned inside out—
The silver tint of the clouds of doubt—

And you never can tell how close you are,
It may be near when it seems afar;

So stick to the fight when you're hardest hit—
It's when things seem worst that you mustn't quit.

We were able to shorten our return hike by a mile or more as ice at the north end of Weasel Cove was thick enough to hold our weight. We crossed there, and then worked our way back to our campsite near the point. It had been twelve hours since we had left. As we walked back toward the shelter, we saw a coast guard cutter circling the bay. Wildly, we ran toward shore, yelling, stumbling, and falling in desperation to get them to see us. The boat went up the channel and right past Weasel Point before disappearing into the fog beyond.

Then we did feel discouraged. Had we listened to the promptings not to start out that day, the boat would have picked us up. If I ever

Chip Porter – 2007

*Ice on Weasel Cove.*

had any doubts that we would be found, it was then. We later learned that the cutter had no real business in the bay. The captain had a new crew and merely came in to acquaint them with the terrain. I am convinced that boat came in answer to prayer. We were not where we should have been or we would have been rescued.

Our clothes were still wet and frozen, so we set to work to make a fire and dry them out. Until our underwear was dry, we had nothing against the arctic cold but the fire. It took all night to get our clothes completely dried out. We fully expected pneumonia. We did not even catch a cold.

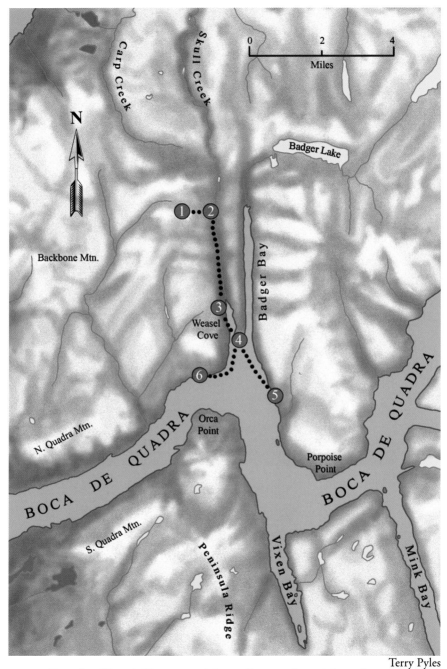

Terry Pyles

*Travels of Joseph Tippets and Percy Cutting from (1) crash site to (2) base camp, (3) Weasel Cove, (4) cabin site at Weasel Point, (5) the cannery, and finally, (6) their attempt to reach open sea.*

*View from cabin site.*

## Chapter Seven
# THE *TUCSAN*

*"I have been going to write a note to you for four weeks.
But I have had, and do have, so much faith that it won't be
long until we are together again that I thought it unnecessary."*

The next couple of days were like a nightmare. We knew we could not go back to our companions. We likely would not make it, and if we did, we would all probably just die there together. All we could do was wait there in hopes that another boat would come in and pick us up. At 11:30 a.m. on Monday, we saw another boat disappear out of the bay. We were heartsick.

Both Sandy and I felt we surely would be picked up on Tuesday. Every day we had said to each other, "This is the day." We talked about the food we most wanted to eat when we were rescued. For Sandy, it was a T-bone steak and all the trimmings or a breakfast of hotcakes and syrup, but my dream was of homemade bread with a chunk of butter in a bowl with hot milk.

We had now been without any food at all for over four days and without a full meal in four weeks. One night, when wolves howled, we took turns watching for them. They had more to fear from us than we had to fear from them. We would have liked nothing better than to get a shot at one.

Chip Porter – 2007

*Mussels.*

During our travels along the shore, we had found some mussels on the beach. We hadn't eaten any before as we knew, down in California, they were sometimes poisonous. But we saw seagulls were eating them and, with our condition being so serious, we decided to try them. If we were going to die, we would at least die with our stomachs full. We built a fire and roasted some. It took a great many to make an ounce of food. When roasted they were about the size of the head of a match. During the night, we kept waking each other up to see if the other was still all right. We fully expected to be poisoned. We did have extreme stomach pains, but we didn't die. The pains were probably the result of a shock to our intestinal systems, from so little food in the past few weeks.

Having survived overnight, we decided to go back down to the rocky beach to get more mussels. That afternoon I wrote a letter to Alta to be found should I die. It is a little bit disjointed, but in a state of exhaustion and frayed emotions, I still tried to convey my love and some key instructions, and to tell her just a little of our story.

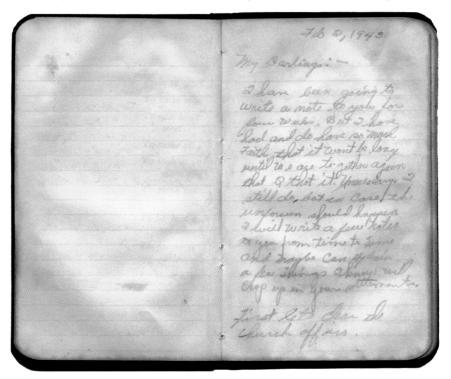

*Notebook, letter to Alta.*

February 2, 1943

My Darlings,

I have been going to write a note to you for four weeks. But I have had, and do have, so much faith that it won't be long until we are together again that I thought it unnecessary. I still do, but in case the unforeseen should happen, I will write a few notes to you from time to time and maybe can explain a few things I know will crop up in your settlements.

First, let's clear up the Church affairs. I have with me

December and January rent money—$90.00. Wells should make it at the settlement. We owe the fast $40.00. Any other shortages have been expended on Church affairs and the Branch should make it up.

At work, I have per diem and other monies coming. I suppose Hop[*] or Plett[**] have explained that to you by now. Also remember I'm on official business and get copies of <u>all</u> letters, telegrams, etcetera, written to me since Dec. 15. Have Mildred Moriarity get them for you. It will help a lot in settling insurance claims.

All my policies are paid up; get Mac[***] to help you legally. I have all our defense bonds, policies and the marriage certificate with me. I had wanted them in Anchorage so I brought them with me. Very foolish, I know. Anyhow, there is the Mutual and the $5,000 Beneficial and the $1,000 Beneficial. You can't get double on any of it, so just collect what you can.

Sell the house to Burton E. Carr out of my department at CAA, $2,400 cash.

Sell the car, $600, to anyone who will buy. Remember, I owe the Bank of Alaska $300.00. I'm sure Mr. Mumford will be lenient until you are financially able to pay him off.

… Try to keep enough money invested so you can give the kids a college education and be sure they both fill <u>missions</u>. (It makes me very tired to write… have had very little to eat for a month now and it's beginning to tell on me.)

As for yourself, dear, I know your judgment is superb. Live close to the Lord and He will always comfort you. He knows you and loves you, so stick to Him. I don't want you to be lonesome and burdened all your life. When you find a companion you would like to have to help you raise the

[*] Marshall C. Hoppin, CAA Alaska Regional Administrator
[**] Walt Plett, CAA Alaska Superintendent of Airways
[***] J. L. McCarrey, LDS friend and attorney

kids, you have my consent to remarry.... You have been my whole life to me. My love for you is life itself, and during these past four weeks I have been buoyed up with my sweet memories of you and our past activities. (I have faith that God is going to see us through this thing, yet.)

I'm going to give you a brief idea of what's happened up to now and you must show this to no one but Hop or Plett and have them come out to the house to read it.

We departed Seattle at 1:30 p.m. Jan. 5 with a taped oil line on the left engine. The pilot had it taped just before taking off in the face of bad weather at Ketchikan. At 6:15 p.m. the left engine quit (no oil...) and we crashed into a mountainside on what we believe is Annette Island.* Sue Batzer, a CAA steno, had her right hand cut off and bled so much she died Thursday, January 7, at 6:30 p.m. The rest of us suffered sprained ankles, bruises, cuts, etcetera except Metzdorf, whose collarbone and some ribs were broken. Gebo had a cracked shinbone, I believe. Sandy Cutting (with me now) had a spinal injury. The pilot (was) unhurt and myself with a bad left ankle and later a frostbitten right foot and many small cuts about the hands. We were fortunate to get out alive. The mountain went straight up and down. Well, we would have been found the next day or so, but the pilot said he had not radioed since Seattle, but had tried to report when the engine went out. So, naturally, no one knew where to look! So we were stuck, cold, wet, hungry, etcetera. We kept camp under one wing (oh yeah, the ship folded up like an accordion... a total wreck!) Well, the pilot left on Sunday to try to bring help (never heard of again). Cold weather, etcetera. The next Saturday, Cutting tried to get out. Spent four days and returned to conserve rations. You can't walk on

* It is likely at this point they definitely knew they were not on Annette and, except for the exhaustion and stress, would have written this sentence in a past tense.

the beach as the rocks drop straight in and you can't walk thru the island out the dense jungle and steep inclines. We don't have the strength... would take two or three days to walk a mile. Well, the misery, cold, hunger and suffering we went thru those three weeks will never be known except by those there. Our emergency rations were limited and very poor as to kind... ."

On that same Tuesday, February 2, two of the brethren in the LDS Anchorage Branch went to see Alta. They later described their memories of that visit:

> I sat in your home in Anchorage and heard and felt Alta's lone but unalterable faith that God had many more and greater accomplishments expected of you in your lifetime... .
> Roy G. Clift

> .... I personally visited Sister Tippets at her humble home. Walking up a wooden walkway to the door of a small cottage... I expressed the sympathies of the membership of the Branch. I will never forget her comments: "Jack, don't you be too concerned because Joseph will yet be found alive." What faith she had.
> John Arrington

I am sure I was being blessed by her faith.

> Midday, on this fateful Tuesday, the *Tucsan*, a small fishing vessel commissioned during the war for service as a Coast Guard Reserve tender, was off Orca Point and picked up a kerosene lantern and fifteen gallons of kerosene, finding nothing else of any value. Then, approaching Kite Island, the crew picked up another kerosene lantern before setting course to Martin Bay Point.

Shortly after 4 p.m. at Martin Bay Point, the crew picked up another kerosene lantern hanging on a tree, then departed for the head of Quadra. Noting that two miles north of Martin Point the rest of Quadra Inlet was frozen up with ice four inches thick, they turned around toward Ketchikan.

Sandy Cutting and I saw the boat about six miles up the bay, seemingly anchored. We began a vigil. We lugged driftwood and branches and we built a pretty good signal fire hoping for a signal back from the boat, but no signal came. We made excuses for their not seeing our fire. We carried wood until our strength was completely gone.

Aboard the *Tucsan*, the boatswain, Augustin W. Angellsen, noted in his log that he had anchored off the Quadra Cannery in twenty feet of water… "light seen on beach at Weasel Cove… believed to be hunters or trappers."

Wednesday, February 3, a blizzard started up about 4 a.m. We couldn't see a thing. At 5 a.m., we built the fire again and at 9 a.m., the storm quit. Everything was white with snow. We couldn't see the boat. We didn't know whether it had gone or not.

On board the *Tucsan*, at 6:30 a.m., heavy snow was falling and they were looking for improved visibility. At 7:00 a.m., the cook was called out and all hands were up at 7:30 a.m. At 8:00 a.m., the deck crew was turned to shoveling snow off the decks, and the log entry was made… "Light at Weasel Cove still burning, believed to be hunters or trappers." The *Tucsan* got underway in Quadra Inlet.

About 9:30 a.m., we had gotten too numb and too weak to keep the fire going and it began to flicker out. We thought that if the ship had gone out, there was no use in having the fire. We turned back into the trees to get out of the bitter wind. Five minutes later, we were both thinking we were hearing something but, at first, neither of us said anything, not wanting to raise false hopes. Our silence, however, didn't last long and we turned to run back to the shore as fast as we could go. We had heard the motors of a boat.

At 9:45 a.m., the *Tucsan* lowered its lifeboat and two men rowed toward the end of Weasel Point. At 9:52 a.m., the log notes "On Weasel Point, one man waving a flag."

We could see it turn in our direction. As it neared the shore, we shouted and waved frantically. I took a couple of quick minutes to go back to our camp and gather up my bundle of books and papers. The coast guard tender had put a lifeboat into the water heading toward us. From the beach, we ran out into the water to meet it. We fell over into the boat almost unconscious.

David Rubin

*The Tucsan Rescue of Tippets and Cutting.*

to return." Alta's statement to a reporter was heartfelt, "To me it was simply an answer to prayer."

## Mrs. Tippets Knew Husband Would Return

"To me it was simply an answer to prayer."

Those were Mrs. Joseph Tippet's words this morning when a Times reporter called to extend congratulations on the word from Ketchikan that her husband was safe and well one month after disappearing into the wilderness of southeastern Alaska with the Harold Gillam plane.

"I had the feeling that Joe was safe," Mrs. Tippets said, "and kept our home and baby as though he were away for a few days and would come home again."

The Tippets baby, 2-year-old John, was born in Anchorage and despite the joy of his father's return is due for a disappointment.

Baby John, since Mr. Tippets left weeks ago to see his mother in Ogden, Utah, has been permitted to share his mother's bed.

So strong was Mrs. Tippets' faith that her husband was somewhere safe and would return, she told friends that it would be difficult to break Baby John's habit of sharing her bed and that she expected the lad to protest when he was returned to his own crib.

Last evening, Mrs. Tippets' joy, she said, was complete when she received a telegram from her husband in Ketchikan. The telegram told her that he was all right except for minor injuries and bruises.

Mr. Tippets is president of the Anchorage branch of the Church of Latter Day Saints of which Mrs. Tippets is also a devout and active member. They have been leaders here in organization and growth of the branch.

In Ogden, Utah, Mr. Tippets' family never gave up hope, an Associated Press story today said.

"We remembered Joe in our prayers," a sister, Mrs. L. R. Priddy said, when advised that her missing brother had been rescued.

"His being found alive makes

### Says She Knew Husband Lived

(Continued from page 1)

us feel just like Eddie Rickenbacker's family," said Mrs. Priddy.

Three other sister and his mother also live in Ogden. Other sisters are Mrs. C. G. Hackett of Montrose, Calif., Mrs. E. C. Fisher of Flint, Mich., and Mrs. V. A. Mahoney of Heber, Utah.

Mrs. Priddy added: "We just couldn't believe Joe was dead in that missing plane after coming here to see Mother who was ill."

Here in Anchorage, Mrs. Tippets has been receiving countless telephone and personal calls from friends, acquaintances and strangers who in a measure shared her happiness.

February 4, 1943, *Anchorage Daily Times*

From the time we reached Ketchikan, the initial hope was to get a rescue mission underway for Dewey Metzdorf and Bob Gebo immediately that evening, but a storm set in and it seemed more advisable to go by boat at night, then start out overland the next morning. Sandy and I prevailed over the doctors in arguing that we could and should participate in the rescue. In hindsight, that probably was foolhardy and this next adventure put our lives at risk again. I had wired Alta that I was alright, except for minor injuries and bruises. What I did not tell her was our plan to lead the rescue. She probably would have understood, but would have had more days of stress and concern. At 4 a.m. Thursday, with frozen feet and aching bodies, we started back.

The initial overland search and rescue was to be made up of about twenty coast guard enlisted personnel led by a crusty chief boatswain,

Art Hook.[*] The *McLane*, a larger coast guard cutter, was designated as the base craft and was sent with the men, food, and implements toward Smeaton Bay. I sailed with the *McLane* while Cutting flew over where we thought we had left Dewey Metzdorf and Bob Gebo. He identified the site, and made repeated passes overhead. Metzdorf

---

# PLANE VICTIMS MAY BE ALIVE

Hope for the safety of Robert Gebo, Seattle construction engineer, was revived today with the news that two of the six persons who vanished on a Seattle-Ketchikan flight four weeks ago were rescued by a Coast Guard patrol boat yesterday.

The two rescued men reported that they had last seen Gebo and another passenger, Dewey Metzdorf of Anchorage, nine days ago. They said that Gego and Metzdorf, who had survived on provisions in the plane, were weakened and suffering from frost-bitten feet, the Associated Press revealed.

A ground searching party headed into the wilderness yesterday, and planes led by Ray Renshaw, Alaska Game Commission pilot, flew over the scene today. A Forest Service plane was to attempt to drop supplies near the wrecked plane and another was to follow the shores of Boca de Quadra Inlet, which Gillam may have been able to reach.

## Camas Woman Killed

The known casualty of the crash against a ridge on the January 3 flight was Susan Batzer, 23 years old, who joined the Alaska Projects of the Civil Aeronautics Administration in Seattle late in December. Before coming to Seattle, Miss Batzer lived with an aunt, Mrs. A. W. Olson, in Camas, Clark County.

The two men rescued were Percy Cutting of Hayward, Calif., an Alaskan employe of Morrison-Knudsen Company, and Joseph Tippits, a Civil Aeronautics Administration employe at Anchorage.

Sixth member of the flight was the pilot, Harold Gillam, veteran Alaskan flyer, who headed southward in search of aid five days after the crash. Gillam, one of Alaska's famous flyers, is known as "Thrill 'em, Spill 'em, No Kill 'em Gillam."

The plane vanished January 3 after Gillam messaged twice within a few minutes that one of his motors was gone.

Gebo, whose home is at 1964 22nd Ave. W., is a graduate of the University of Washington and general superintendent for Morrison-Knudsen Company, operators of the plane. Morrison-Knudsen Company, a construction firm with headquarters in Boise, Idaho, holds large contracts in Alaska.

February 4, 1943, *The Seattle Times*

---

came out and waved as the pilot dipped his wing to confirm he had seen them. They dropped blankets and food; one bundle fell too far into the woods where Metzdorf was unable to retrieve it, but he did

---

*Arthur Hook had been a commercial diver before the war. In December 1942, to reach a crashed plane that had carried important mail, he smashed through ice in Juneau's Gastineau Channel. Diving more than one hundred feet, he retrieved the pilot's body and the classified mail. (J. Leahy, *The Coast Guard at War in Alaska*, in *Alaska at War*, ed. F. Chandonnet, p. 128.)

get to the second one. It wasn't clear at that moment if there was only one survivor or two. Sandy was flown to the *McLane* and joined me on board.

USCG – 1943

*The rescue group onboard the McLane prior to going ashore—*
*Joe Tippets is at top of picture (face in profile).*

From a landing site on the shore of Smeaton Bay, Sandy directed the shore party overland toward the camp. With snow three to five feet deep the going was exhausting. It was a treacherous and difficult hike for eleven and a half hours into and through the night. We fired guns into the air and our party scattered out in search of Metzdorf and Gebo, but we were frustrated in not finding them. We finally made camp at 10:30 p.m. and two groups alternated resting and maintaining the fire.

*U.S. Coast Guard party, February 4, en route to find Gebo and Metzdorf.*
*(fifth in column is Joseph Tippets)*

The following morning at daybreak, February 5, we discovered that in the darkness we had missed the camp where we had left our companions by just about 300 yards. It was thirty-one days after the crash. Bob and Dewey were in bad condition, lying in thawing snow water surrounded by snow three feet deep. They had become too weak to move from the pine bough bedding and the lean-to canvas covering or to reach the fire and fuel it with the wood we had left them. To pass the time and keep up their spirits, they talked about plans to open a new hotel and restaurant together once they were rescued. But hope was gradually fading and they were also preparing for death, placing their official identification cards in their hatbands. Seeing Bob and Dewey in this pitiful condition caused lumps in the throats of their rescuers. In relief, Bob and Dewey broke into tears as did Sandy and I. We were blubbering, but there was no reason to be embarrassed for doing so. Others wiped tears from their eyes as well.

Dewey said, "I don't know how I did it, but I mustered enough strength to crawl out, stand up, and wave to your pilot when he came over our camp yesterday. If he hadn't dipped his wings as a signal that he saw me, I couldn't have made it to Bob's side. I would have died right there." Bob described that his toes were now totally numb and he was unable to stand.

# Fire Went Out, Survivors Lay In Snow Water

## Metzdorf and Gebo Were Too Weak To Move From Tent

Robert Gebo and Dewey Metzdorf for several days lay in thawing snow water without a fire as they awaited rescue, they told Chief Warrant Officer Art Hook, who led the first coast guard party to reach the injured plane crash survivors.

Too weak to move from their pallets in the canvas lean-to in which Joseph H. Tippets and Percy Cutting left them, the injured pair could not reach the fire a few feet away to fuel it with the wood which Tippets and Cutting cut for them.

### PLANE SAW HIM

"I just had strength enough to crawl out, stand up and wave to that pilot when he came over our camp," Metzdorf told Hook. "If he hadn't dipped his wings as a signal that he saw me, I couldn't have made it back to Gebo's side. I would have died right there."

The flyer Metzdorf referred to was Ray Renshaw, who dropped supplies to the men last Thursday.

"Their camp was surrounded by snow—about five feet deep," Hook said. "A stream of melting slush ran right under and around them. They alternately thawed and froze as the weather changed.

### MEN CHEERFUL

"When we saw them, lying there soaking wet but grinning, we just cried like babies. We couldn't help it. Seeing what those men had been through was too much for all of us. Everybody wept, Gebo and Metzdorf and I and the rest of the men."

As Gebo and Metzdorf lay in their sopping, icy blankets they took turns massaging each other's body to keep from freezing. It was the only way they could maintain any circulation.

February 8, 1943, *Ketchikan Alaska Chronicle*

At this point, having expended our last physical strength, and with the emotional catharsis of seeing our friends, any adrenaline we might have been calling on was gone. It was obvious to all that Sandy and I, exhausted and still in a state of shock from our own trials of the past month, needed to be taken back to the *McLane* as soon as possible. Most of the rescue party would remain behind to work with Gebo and Metzdorf to provide medical attention, build their strength, and to develop a careful plan and process to extricate them.

USCG – 1943

*Metzdorf, after being found, is made more comfortable.*

Bob Gebo requested that, when I got back to the *McLane*, I tell them, "We can last it out here forever. Now we have food and know they have seen us. We're fine, just fine. It was the grandest day of my life when that plane dropped that food." In his capacity as Alaska general superintendent for Morrison-Knudsen, Bob also told me to authorize any expense in the search for Harold Gillam. I assured him that the Alaska Coast Guard commandant had already ordered un-limited measures to be taken in the search.

USCG – 1943

*Joseph Tippets after finding Gebo and Metzdorf.*

When Art Hook asked for volunteers to accompany us back down the trail, two young coast guardsmen, William C. Wade and Bruce L. White, stepped forward. We can't say too much for them. That trip was almost our death once again. Rain had made the snow slushy and walking was a great agony, but they pushed us, prodded us, and pulled us. We came to a stream which had been frozen on our way up, but was thawed and impassable on the way back. We just sat down

Ensign J. J. Casby – 1943, courtesy of Alan Casby

*Tippets and Cutting returning to the McLane.*

and cried. Those boys practically carried us across. Halfway back, our party met up with Dan Ralston, the Game Commission agent and Gene Gull, a CAA inspector, who were hoping to proceed up the mountain to the site of the wreckage. Gull and Ralston, however, turned back with our exhausted party to help us. It took seven and a half hours to get us back out, reaching the beach about 6 p.m. and signaling the vessel for a small boat to come get us.

Our first report to the captain in coming on board was to express appreciation for White and Wade, for their pluck and endurance. They saved our lives (again). As we sat that night to eat in the officer's ward room, Sandy said that since the breakfast in Seattle on January 5, this "is my first hot meal in a month." I corrected him, however. "I beg your pardon," I said. "Those crows I roasted were hot!"

Sandy and I were soon transferred to a small boat to be sent to Ketchikan, but the Alaska winter was not quite finished with us. The boat had no sooner left when an extremely heavy snow squall struck. The skipper of our boat was concerned, so rather than take any risk, he returned alongside the *McLane*. We were then transferred to a larger vessel, the *Sebanus* and finally made our way to Ketchikan, where we were immediately put back in the hospital.

Meanwhile, another coast guard shore party carrying more sleeping bags, waterproof tarpaulins, food, tools, and medicine was pushing up the tortuous trail to the valley camp. That night, Art made up a mulligan stew with corned beef. Twenty-plus men had their stew and slice of bread while sharing four service kits. Hook also decided there was little point in sending anyone up the mountain to the crash site itself. Instead, work parties should be put to building bridges across the flooded streams. The pharmacist's mates treated Bob and Dewey. Others cut firewood to create a large bonfire, and bundles of supplies were dropped during the day from three different planes out of Ketchikan.

While we had been going in to find Bob and Dewey and then returning to the *McLane*, actions were underway to prepare to bring them out. A USN "Kingfisher" had done aerial reconnaissance to determine alternative ways out to the water. Scouting the terrain, a local woodsman and trapper, Bruce Johnstone, recommended the ships come to Badger Bay Inlet off Boca de Quadra. Badger Bay was a deep arm, but it was fed by several freshwater creeks and the surface of the inlet was frozen over. The Kingfisher dropped bombs to try to break the ice, but that did not do the job. The *Mighty Mac* had to become an icebreaker, breaking through ice in some places fourteen inches thick. They were worried about damage as the ship plowed ahead, then backed off in making several successive charges until reaching a point close to shore to set up an operating base.[6] A group of the local territorial guards, experienced in dealing with the Alaska winter, set out to the base camp to support the coast guard personnel.

USCG – 1943

*The Wildlife Services Game Commission patrol boat, Ranger, in Badger Bay. (Picture likely taken from the McLane.)*

On Friday and Saturday, efforts were focused on making the two survivors strong. A new shelter was built, the men's beds were raised off the ground, the pharmacist's mates labored over them, and fires were built and sustained. The men ate sandwiches, shared a can of fruit, and enjoyed some warm coffee. Additional planes flew over and dropped blankets and sleeping bags. They didn't have walkie-talkies, so messages were conveyed from the ground by using red bunting or by tracking words on the snow. They requested saws, axes, tarpaulins, buckets, and so forth.

[6]J. Gill, *Before the Whirley Birds.*

USCG – 1943

*Needs, requests were conveyed from the ground by tracking messages in the snow.*

USCG – 1943

*Rescuers at new camp.*

USCG – 1943
*Territorial Guardsman, Bruce Johnstone, with USCG Pilots.*
*Lt. Comdr. Joseph F. McCue (center) and Ensign James P. Gwynn (right).*

USCG – 1943
*The U.S. Coast Guard Grumman Goose dropped supplies*
*to shore party caring for Metzdorf and Gebo.*

97

By Sunday morning (day 33), there were eighteen inches of fresh snow. Nine of the rescue team, having bad ankles, frostbitten feet,

Dewey Metzdorf, Jr.
*Dewey's lucky Dachshund*

sprained wrists, or other ailments, started out ahead as they would not be helpful with the Gebo/Metzdorf team. A sled was built from two trees and a wire basket for Bob was placed on top. Dewey Metzdorf was placed in an improvised toboggan. He carried with him the little ceramic dachshund, intact except for a piece broken off the tail.

USCG – 1943

*Rescue crew with toboggan carrying Metzdorf.*

Four or five men led the way and about fifteen were with the sled and the toboggan. They pulled along, lowered, or held back as the terrain demanded. At times the rescuers had to form a human chain to ease the two men down slopes. Sailors from the *McLane*, coast guardsmen, and the local members of the territorial guard were participating, taking turns on the sleds and/or scouting ahead for the best trail to avoid holes in the snowdrifts. It was an exhausting seven and a half hours until they reached the Badger Bay shoreline, where another rescue group, including medical personnel, joined them. From there, it was out over the ice to the ship. Luckily, the path the *McLane* had cut through the ice had not frozen over and the ship was able to make its way back out into clear water and then back to Ketchikan.

Gebo and Metzdorf, after thirty-three harrowing days in extreme cold and isolation, suffering the agony of broken bones, severe frostbite, near starvation, in a constant confrontation with potential death, were safe and would in due time return to their families. Their courage, endurance, and faith provide yet another miracle in this whole episode. As Bob and Dewey were being rescued, the "Send Blimp" and toboggan pictures and story reached newspapers across the country, including the *New York Times*.

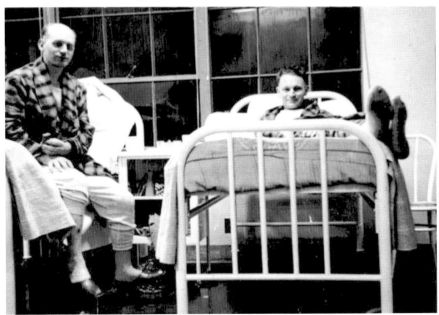

USCG

*Joseph Tippets and "Sandy" Cutting*
*in Ketchikan hospital.*

Sandy Cutting and I had been back in the hospital in Ketchikan and obviously out of the excitement for those couple of days as Bob Gebo and Dewey Metzdorf were treated and then brought out of their wilderness camp. We had been anguished for them as we were being interviewed about our experiences. Sandy said, "Gebo and Metzdorf are the ones who have had the most terrible time. They have had to stay behind and wait." They were without food for days until the plane dropped the food supplies to them on Thursday. Sandy and I were now beginning to recover, eat, and with the help of sedatives, we were able to get some rest. I did tell someone to have my wife please wire me to tell me how she was and how Johnny was, and to tell her I was swell.

A local Ketchikan member of my church thoughtfully brought me some clean clothes, which I very much appreciated. I also took a moment to write to my mother, in part, "You'll never know how my memories and the teachings you have given me have helped the past month. I've just lived by them."

In Ogden, Utah, for the whole duration of my ordeal, my mother had remained in bed at the home of her daughter, Alice, seriously ill in a semi-conscious state. My sisters carefully avoided talking about the plane crash in her presence, yet, they reported, she seemed to know something and, on one occasion, suddenly woke up and described me as being lost and in trouble, needing ropes and help. Mother also seemed determined to live until I was safe. Three days after I was rescued, she peacefully passed away. My sister, Mary Mahoney, wrote:

> And one day Mama said, "They're going to find Joe today." We didn't even know she knew he was lost because she had been so unconscious. She said, "Joe's going to find himself, but he's alright and we're going to find him." And sure enough, when they later found him, why, that was the day that he did go for help and got found. And as soon as she decided that Joe was all right, she died (on February 6, 1943).

During the process of evacuating Gebo and Metzdorf, another search party on board the *Cedar*, an Alaska Game Commission vessel, discovered the body of Harold Gillam along the shoreline of another

# Last Survivors Of Plane Crash Brought Here

## Metzdorf and Gebo in Hospital With Cutting and Tippets

Safe at last after 33 horrible days in the wilderness, Dewey Metzdorf and Robert Gebo lay in the coast guard hospital here today in a room adjoining that occupied by Percy Cutting and Joseph H. Tippets, the other two survivors of the plane crash which eventually cost the lives of Pilot Harold Gillam and Susan Batzer.

Gillam's body was brought to Ketchikan late Saturday afternoon. It was found 150 feet above the tide line near Weasel cove by searchers on an Alaska game commission vessel.

Miss Batzer's body still lies in the wreckage of the plane on the precipitous mountainside where the tragic saga had its beginning on January 5. How soon woodsmen will be able to scale the steep, 2000-foot cliff and reach the plane is unknown. Deep winter snowdrifts and almost impassable, heavily forested terrain will make the task exceeding difficult, according to members of the party which brought Gebo and Metzdorf to safety.

Experienced civilian woodsmen and guides aided the coast guard yesterday in bringing Metzdorf and Gebo from their valley camp at the foot of the mountain on which the plane crashed. After a wide trail had been cut from the head of Badger bay to the camp, the rescuers were able to bring the injured men to the beach in two and a half hours. Gebo was lashed to a toboggan; Metzdorf was carried on a wire stretcher which was lashed to a sled made of cedar poles.

### BONE MENDED

So much time elapsed between the crash and the rescue that Metzdorf's broken collarbone knitted together. He also suffered several broken ribs in the crash. Placed under a physician's care as soon as he was taken aboard a coast guard cutter at the beach, he was discovered also to be suffering from severely frostbitten fingers and toes. Greeted by his wife, who came here by steamer from the south, the once portly Anchorage hotel owner was so overcome by emotion and exhaustion that he could not speak. Tears rolled down his cheeks as Mrs. Metzdorf embraced him.

Gebo, not as strong as Metzdorf and more seriously injured, exhibited superhuman endurance, as did all the survivors. His right leg was broken and both feet badly frostbitten. But both men were in excellent spirits, despite their torturous trial. As Metzdorf was being transferred from his stretcher to a small boat yesterday, he turned to his companion and grinned, "How ya doing, pal?"

Thus the most intensive rescue search in the history of this area drew to a close. While exhausted members of the searching parties rested today, others made plans to return to the mountain as soon as conditions permit to obtain Miss Batzer's body. The shattered plane, a snowy tomb for a brave girl, may be left on the mountainside. The survivors' reports indicate that only a few of the instruments are worth salvaging.

February 8, 1943, *Ketchikan Alaska Chronicle*

arm of Boca de Quadra on February 6. Morrison-Knudsen had put up a reward and about 200 men were out looking for him. Harold was found about 150 feet above the tide line by Jack Johnstone, Fish and Game Warden, Joe Lynch, and Dr. Siders, USPHS medical officer. Jack Johnstone was the brother of Bruce, engaged at the time in the evacuation. The location was about three miles northeast of Quadra Point directly across from Boca Point.[7] He had made an effort to put up a signal with a strip of red cloth and his boots on poles. All of us were sad at the fate of Harold. He was a strong man—in physique, courage, and spirit—and he certainly did everything it was possible for a human being to do for us. He died probably as he would have preferred it—on the job, struggling for the welfare of his passengers.*

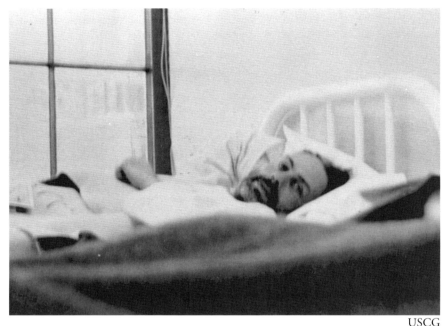

USCG

*Dewey Metzdorf in Ketchikan hospital.*

After being rescued, Bob Gebo gave his own account of his brush with death. "We felt like redeemed souls. Only one who has faced the prospect of death can know the joy of a reprieve. I could not let myself think again of taking for granted creature comforts like soft

[7] *The Coast Guard at War: Transports and Escorts.* May 1, 1949 (CGC McLane).
*Onboard the *Cedar*, a Game Commission patrol boat, was Captain Burns, Dr. Siders, and others. A local territorial guard, Ken Eichner, put himself in the bow to look for signs of Gillam. "We had gone a few miles into the Quadra when I spotted an orange streamer hanging from a bare yellow cedar tree.… Captain Burns sent Jack Johnstone and Joe Lynch, Fish and Game Warden, ashore. They soon found Harold Gillam's body. He had made the nearly impossible trek from the wreck to this point.… Overextended and in a weakened condition, he had hung the streamer and rolled himself up in his parachute.… The memory still haunts me of the black beard of the first victim I had ever seen." (K. Eichner, *Nine Lives of an Alaska Bush Pilot*, p. 34.)

beds, warm rooms, hunger appeased… as I had done in the past. Best of all, I could now look forward to seeing my wife and young son again." He described the physical impact on Metzdorf and himself of the thirty-one days. "From a veritable giant of 220 pounds, Dewey Metzdorf had dwindled down to a bony 160. I, who had been definitely husky at 190, was practically a shadow at 140. But the important thing is that we are alive: we shall be well and we shall be able to live useful lives." As a consequence of the gangrene he suffered, all of Bob's toes were amputated and, in fact, doctors also had to rebreak his leg to allow it to heal correctly.

Now only one of our fellow passengers in the crash remained in the mountain wilderness—Susan Batzer's body there in the fuselage of the Lockheed Electra. On February 15, a group of six men set out to retrieve her. The party consisted of Gene Gull, a senior inspector for the CAA, the two local woodsmen Bruce and Jack Johnstone, and three coast guardsmen. They spent the first night at the base camp where Gebo and Metzdorf had been nursed toward recovery. Going up the mountain the next day, they reached the plane at 1 p.m. Due to recent heavy rains, the snow level around the crash site had receded to five or six feet, less than half of what it had been a week or two prior. Most of the group worked to assemble a sled and remove Susan's body from the plane. Gene Gull inspected the airplane, finding charts and records and retrieving some of the instruments. The group then made its way back down the mountain to the base camp. The next day, they made it to the shore and the coast guard brought them into Ketchikan at about 8:30 p.m. We now had closure for all six of us who had been on that ill-fated flight. Susan's body was subsequently returned to the States and she was buried in Camas, Washington.

The men who discovered Harold's body made the decision to donate the $1,500 reward to his children.

*Joseph and Alta.*

## Chapter Nine
# WE WERE NOT ALONE

*"I was grateful to the Coast Guard, for the efforts on our behalf by the Morrison-Knudsen Company, and even more for the faith, prayers, and support of friends and family."*

I n those twenty-nine days that I was lost, I came to a fuller appreciation of the worth and true character in man. The hundreds of little ways we each tried to make another of our group more comfortable, or to assist with their needs, to be tolerant and considerate of the others' views and opinions, all contributed to the preserving of our strength and ability to think clearly. I realized, as never before, that no matter how much money a man has in the bank, or how well he is doing, or how big a job he has, nothing really counts but character. Although we were constantly battling the weather and were frustrated in nearly all our efforts to find rescue, there is one thing we never did—give up hope. It seemed as though we were constantly strengthened to keep up our spirits and to somehow replenish our bodies with energy. Bob Gebo also marveled, "Through those weeks of constant exposure to the worst the elements could heap upon us, no one even caught a cold. For one thing, the temperature was pretty uniform—always cold. Another thing that was a great help were those ABC vitamins that

Dewey's wife had put in his luggage. Each of us took two capsules a day, so although our diet was woefully lacking in calories, we did receive our daily requirement of vitamins."[9]

The amazing thing, of course, is that we are alive. None of us can account for our having been spared. After enduring so much, we can only thank God for preserving us. It seems we must have been brought through for some purpose—that we each may have some assignments to fulfill before we pass on. I hope I will never lose this thought.

I finally returned to Anchorage on February 20, two months after originally setting out for Seattle and Utah. As I was interviewed by a reporter for the *Anchorage Daily Times*, I described how extremely thankful I was to be alive. It was hard to understand why we four had survived the crash while Susan had not, and how it was that Harold, as experienced as he was, perished trying to bring rescue to us. I expressed gratitude for the coast guard, for the efforts on our behalf by the Morrison-Knudsen Company, and even more for the faith, prayers, and support of friends and family.

*Joe and Alta returning at Merrill Field, Anchorage.*

A February 1943 editorial in *The Alaska Fishing News*, well summarized those difficult weeks and put our experiences into the context of World War II in which America and all Americans were then engaged:

[9]E. Dawson and R. Gebo, *The Gillam Plane Was Missing*, in *Alaska Sportsman*, July 1943.

RY 8, 1943.     *THE ALASKA FISHING NEWS*

FEBRUARY 8, 1943

EDITORIAL

Heroism is not confined to the roar of battle alone.

In quiet places, in civilian life, far removed from strife and excitement of war, may be found examples of unselfish deeds, with no thought of reward.

No greater saga of the Northland was ever recounted than the experiences of the survivors of the Gillam plane crash.

Bruised, shaken up, injured in the crash landing, with a scant supply of food, in freezing sub-Arctic weather, each and every one unselfishly co-operated for the common good.

Terrible privation and hardship for over a month did not cause one of them to "crack" or complain.

The first victim, Susan Baltzer, 25, a young woman in the prime of life, on her first trip to Alaska, tenderly cared for, died from loss of blood and shock, without a single complaint.

Harold Gillam, veteran Alaska pilot, the second victim, though injured, lost his life in going for help.

Percy Cutting and Joseph H. Tippets, also injured, set out to get help, leaving behind what little food there was, and taking along a 22 calibre rifle. Before that Cutting made a several days' search and returned to camp. Dewey Metzdorf was left at camp, when the two men left, to rustle wood for a fire and take care of Robert Gebo, who suffered a broken leg.

Tippets and Cutting forded icy streams, slipped around cliffs and ploughed through snow to reach tidewater. They were several days without food, living on a raven they shot and mussels, taking to the water in an improvised raft which sunk under them and then in a leaky boat they found which sunk, compelling them to swim ashore. When found, though exhausted and nearly starving, they wanted the crew of the boat to take them at once to their companions. Then, on refusal, because of their condition, after a few hours hospitalization in Ketchikan, they insisted on returning to the scene of the crash with rescuers. That put them back in the hospital.

Pilot Gillam and Susan Batzer died in the "line of duty" as truly as any soldier on the battlefield.

The extreme heroism and endurance of the survivors thrills us with pride. They are Americans, the exemplification of that American spirit to the highest degree which is winning the war on the many battle fronts.

A spirit such as theirs gives us supreme confidence that democracy must and will prevail.

*"Welcome Home."*

It was a joyful reunion with my wife and son, little Johnny. I was surprised by his now extensive vocabulary; he talked a blue streak, which he didn't when I left. But it was heartbreaking to learn that Alta had lost the new baby. I gained a deeper appreciation of how anxious and stressful the whole experience had been for her. About this same time, I wrote a letter of condolence to Susan's parents, Mr. and Mrs. H.W. "Winch" Batzer, of Idaho Falls. I wanted to express the admiration we all felt for Susan and to give them a more complete account of the crash.*

As we returned to Anchorage, the words of CAA Regional Manager, Marshall C. Hoppin, reflected the feelings of our friends and associates:

> When the Morrison Knudsen plane, with its six passengers, was lost on January 5, we were all concerned. When the plane had been missing for days, our concerns changed to anxiety… and after weeks had passed, we gradually grew discouraged and hopeless and felt that never again would we see our lost friends and acquaintances.
>
> We all remember the almost incredulous joy and amazement we experienced on February 3 upon hearing that two survivors had been found, including our good friend and coworker, Joseph H. Tippets. After a month of privation and suffering, the fact that even four of the six on board the ill-fated plane survived the long, miserable month almost taxes our imagination, and proves indeed that faith and hope and courage and endurance have tangible rewards.
>
> The age of miracles is not past!

*See Appendix A.
[10]M. C. Hoppin, Mukluk Telegraph, March, 1943.

I also received a much appreciated personal letter from the First Presidency of the Church. They expressed gratitude for my rescue, their concern, and prayers for a full recovery of my health and their wishes for our Heavenly Father's continued blessings.

In March, we went back to Ogden, Utah for a rest. One of the first people I went to see was Brother Jesse Draper. I made it a point to see Brother Draper because my first elementary knowledge of splints and bandages and fires had been from his training as my scoutmaster. I

*Jesse H. Draper*

could remember him carefully putting his arms around me and helping me with a fire or to make a stretcher. And he especially emphasized keeping "dry matches!" I didn't know it at the time, but Brother Draper was very ill and passed away a few weeks later. I was grateful I could go back and thank him for his patience and his teachings.

Looking back on this whole experience and recognizing all of those to whom I owe thanks, I am reminded of the words of Richard L. Evans, in one of his *Spoken Word* pieces reprinted in *Unto the Hills*, which I carried with me those twenty-nine days:

> Men who think they pursue their lives independently of all outside forces are as foolish as the seaman who thinks he pilots his ship alone, when he steers by the stars in the heavens and takes his bearings from maps and instruments that centuries and generations have produced. No man is a law unto himself. His mother bears him; families and friends and society rear him from infancy; other men teach

him, make the clothes he wears, provide the food he eats, and run the world he lives in; and God who is in heaven crosses his path with influence and impressions. Let no man play the fool and glory in his own self-sufficiency, for no man lives who is self-sufficient.

In my heart, I knew we were not alone.

# EPILOGUE

*"We each have some assignments to fulfill before we pass on."*

Deseret News

*Alta and Joseph with the Scriptures and the book Unto the Hills, which miraculously also survived the twenty-nine-day adventure.*

I n the weeks following the rescue of the passengers on the Gillam plane, Joseph Tippets was given several opportunities to describe his experiences to the news media. He was interviewed by the *Anchorage Daily Times*, the *Salt Lake City Deseret News*, the *Ogden* (Utah) *Standard Examiner* and newspapers in Ketchikan and

Cordova, Alaska. The *Cordova Daily Times* story, "Survivor Tells of Wilderness Peninsula Plane Crash," published on March 8, 1943 is one of the more complete accounts. Sometime later, his first-person account of the ordeal (originally in *The Improvement Era*, November, 1943) was included in *LDS Adventure Stories,* compiled by Preston Nibley. He was quoted by Jean Potter in her classic book, *The Flying North* (1945) and also mentioned in *Sea Drift*, the memoirs of F.A. Zeusler (1980), who was the coast guard subsector commander in Alaska in 1943, and who organized the search for the missing plane. Over the years, my dad was asked to share his story with many audiences, including church "firesides," two of which were tape-recorded. And, finally, we have the small notebook he had with him on the mountain and the letter he wrote in pencil to my mother, Alta, in case they didn't find rescue. Each of the accounts have small variations, but the differences are not significant, and I have tried to reconcile them in this text.

Always, in telling his story, Dad was extremely aware and grateful for his miraculous survival and rescue, and consciously tried for the next twenty-five years to live and serve in a manner worthy of what he believed was the Lord's intervention on his behalf. A couple of weeks after his rescue, in a letter of gratitude to the First Presidency of the LDS Church, he wrote in part:

> …. I had never been cold or hungry—to such an extent of discomfort—before. Now knowing these things and having to live on only that which was provided from prayer, I testify to the divinity of our work—and that the Lord does hear us and answer our prayers. Our lives now are at the disposal of our fellowmen, as they have been always.
>
> The Lord has been kind to us and we do appreciate it—now that my life has been spared under such miraculous circumstances—we feel more than ever our responsibilities to the Lord and the Church.

In giving all he could to "God and country," Joseph rose through the ranks of the Civil Aeronautics Administration, transferring from Alaska to Washington, D.C. in 1947. He represented the United States in several international aviation forums in the 1950s, where air navigation standards were established. He was also extensively involved in the initial planning/development for Dulles International Airport. The CAA became the Federal Aviation Agency (FAA) and Joseph reached the highest levels of civil service responsibilities as the FAA Western Region director, based in Los Angeles (1961-1967) and returning to Washington, D.C., where in 1967 and 1968 he was the associate administrator of the FAA for personnel and training.

CAA – 1950s

*Joseph Tippets.*

During the years after the Morrison-Knudsen crash, Joseph's love of aviation never diminished. In October 1946, he actually survived an additional serious accident at Manley Hot Springs in central Alaska on the Tanana River, about 100 miles west of Fairbanks. The Twin Beech was destroyed, but Joseph, sitting in the copilot's seat, described himself as having "no injuries but my pride." He was also

CAA – 1946

*Crash at Manley Hot Springs.*

involved in a minor incident, a blown tire on a DC-3 taking off from Merrill Field in Anchorage. Finally fulfilling a life-long ambition in the 1960s, Joseph took flight instruction in Los Angeles, and earned his pilot's license with a multi-engine rating. Just for fun, he also flew as a copilot in a T-33 "T-Bird" jet trainer.

In his LDS Church callings, Dad continued as the Anchorage Branch president until 1947, then served as the bishop of the Capitol Ward (1949-1953), as a member of the Washington, D.C. stake presidency (1957-1961), and in other church responsibilities.

Elder Neal A. Maxwell, in his book, *A More Excellent Way*, described his friend Joe Tippets:

> Anyone who knows Joseph Tippets of the Federal Aviation Agency is privileged to know one of the great men of the Church. Joe's total commitment gives him a constancy and authenticity that never fails to come across. In a world of chameleons, this is the constancy of the character Jesus Christ would have us to pursue. His authenticity, combined with his love and openness, far from offending others, finds them admiring him openly....[11]

A wonderful and unexpected highlight of Dad's long career in government and church service came in May, 1967 when he was awarded an Honorary Doctorate Degree of Public Service from

[11]Neal. A. Maxwell, A More Excellent Way, 1967, p. 137.

114

Brigham Young University. FAA colleagues and employees of his Western Region had written letters to BYU nominating him for this honor. The citation presented at this time concluded:

> In recognition of his achievements in aviation development, for the integrity, dedication, and leadership ability he has displayed in the service of the United States of America, and for his lifelong dedication to public service… Joseph H. Tippets is awarded the degree of Doctor of Public Service, *honoris causa*.

*Joseph H. Tippets and Ernest L. Wilkinson, President,*
*with Ben E. Lewis, Executive Vice President, Brigham Young University.*

All who came into contact with Joseph Tippets over those ensuing twenty-five years were impacted by his energy and his love for people. His attitude toward life can be seen in the following words he wrote to a young missionary:

… The gospel is not only for the hereafter, but surely the beauty, the purpose, and the joys which it gives us in this life are of equal importance. Oft'times, we emphasize the great distant future, which I agree is very important, but *today* is important, too. I wonder if we always appreciate the exalted position in which our souls are placed in this life for our sincere testimony and desire to be of service to our Heavenly Father. So many times our people say that we must do this or that today because it will be of importance after we die. Surely, it will be important after we die, but after all, it is awfully important before we die, too. It has often been said by many that they would be willing to die for the gospel, but probably it is even more important that we live for the gospel. By this, I mean to live every day and enjoy it to its fullest, letting the tomorrows take care of themselves, as they will do if we only take good care of today.[12]

Joseph Tippets died on October 18, 1968. At his funeral, David Thomas, his longtime friend and colleague, who was at that time the acting Administrator of the Federal Aviation Administration, told this story:

I was back in the bush in Alaska and an old grizzled prospector came up to me and said, "I hear you're from Washington, D.C." I said, "I am." He said, "It's a big town, isn't it?" and I said, "Yes, it's a big town." He said, "It's probably so large you never heard of a man named Joe Tippets. He was the finest man that was ever in Alaska."

Given the opportunity, Dad would have described the prospector as having had too small a sample. However, many others who knew and loved Joe Tippets might say that prospector was right.

[12]Joseph H. Tippets, in a letter to Elder Bob Goodman, September 1, 1953.

Our mother died in 1973. Joseph and Alta are buried in the Heber City Cemetery, Wasatch County, Utah. They are survived by my two brothers, David and Robert, our sister, Marilyn Stanger, and me, as well as eighteen grandchildren.

*John M. Tippets*

Note: Dewey Metzdorf passed away in Palm Springs, California in 1966 at the age of sixty-seven, Percy "Sandy" Cutting at Reno, Nevada in 1977 at the age of seventy-five, and Robert Gebo in San Mateo, California in 1981 at the age of seventy-four.

# RESOURCES

## Newspapers

*Anchorage Daily Times*. January–February 1943.

Cutting, Percy and Joseph Tippets. "Survivors' Story of Twenty-Nine-Day Struggle against Death." *Ketchikan Alaska Chronicle* February 6, 1943.

*Idaho Falls Post Register*. February 1943.

*Ketchikan Alaska Chronicle* and *Ketchikan Daily News*. January–February 1943.

*Ketchikan Daily News*. "1943: Bush Pilot's Career Ends in Boca de Quadra." February 8, 1993.

*Ketchikan Daily News*. "1943 Gillam Crash Ended Epic Alaska Flying Career." January 2003. 60th-year- anniversary article.

*Ogden Standard Examiner*. "Amazing Faith in Survival Revealed in Plane Accident." March 12, 1943.

*Ogden Standard Examiner*. "Only Yesterday; 20 Years Ago." January 31, 1963.

*Seattle Times*. January–February 1943.

*The Alaska Fishing News*. February 8, 1943.

*The Cordova Daily Times*. "Survivor Tells of Wilderness Plane Crash." March 8, 1943.

*The Deseret News*. "Answers to Prayers." March 7, 1943.

The Hayward Review. January–February 1943.

## Books

Bruder, Gerry. *Heroes of the Horizon*. Alaska Northwest Books, 1991.

Chandonnet, Fern, ed. *Alaska at War*. "The Forgotten War Remembered" (papers from the Alaska at War Symposium, Anchorage, Alaska, November, 11-13, 1993).

Cloe, John H. *The Aleutian Warriors: A History of the Eleventh Air Force and Fleet Air Wing 4*. Anchorage Chapter, "Air Force Association and Pictorial Histories." Publishing Company,. First printing June 1991.

Eichner, Kenneth. *Nine Lives of an Alaska Bush Pilot*. Taylor Press, 2002.

Evans, Richard. L. *Unto the Hills*. Harper and Brothers, 1940.

Garfield, Brian. *The Thousand-Mile War: World War II in Alaska and the Aleutians*. University of Alaska Press edition, 1995 (originally published in 1969).

Grant, R.G.; Summers, David, DK Project Editor, and Smithsonian

National Air and Space Museum. *Flight: 100 Years of Aviation*. DK Publishing, 2002.

Griese, Arnold. *Bush Pilot*. Publication Consultants, 2005.

Nibley, Preston, comp. "Alaskan Rescue" in *LDS Adventure Stories*. Bookcraft, 1953.

Potter, Jean. *The Flying North*. Comstock, 1st ed. 1945.

Wilson, John R.M. *Turbulence Aloft: The Civil Aeronautics Administration amid Wars and Rumors of Wars, 1938-1953*. U.S. Department of Transportation, Washington, D.C., 1979.

Zeusler, F.A. "Air-Sea Rescue in Alaska," in *Sea Drift*, Vantage Press, 1980.

## Magazines

Cutting, Percy, and Kathryn Eckroth. "Hell in God's Country." *Alaska Life: The Territorial Magazine* August 1943.

Dassow, Ethel and Robert Gebo. "The Gillam Plane Was Missing." *Alaska Sportsman*, Vol. IX, no. 7, July 1943: 16-18, 21-22. (Also in *Alaska Adventures*, Vol. 1 No. 1.)

*FAA Horizons*, "They Cheated Icy Death." October 14, 1968.

Markham, Ira J., and Joseph H. Tippets. "Alaskan Rescue." *The Improvement Era* October 1943.

Rypinski, Arthur, TIGHAR #2548. "The Men Did Their Duty: The Story of the Ketchikan Electra Crash." *TIGHAR Tracks (The Journal of the International Group for Historic Aircraft Recovery)*, Vol. 20 #3 December 2004: 9-27.

Morrison-Knudsen. *The Em Kayan* 1942 and 1943 issues.

"Alaska Plane Crash Tragedy and Rescue: An Epic of Faith and Heroism in the Frozen North." *The Em Kayan* March 1943.

"The Year of the Dado (The Earhart Project)" and "The Ketchikan Wreck." *TIGHAR Tracks (The Journal of the International Group for Historic Aircraft Recovery)* Vol. 20 #3 December 2004: 6-8.

Zeusler, F. A. "Air Sea Rescue in Alaska." *Coast Guard Alumni Association Bulletin*, January-February 1961.

## Other

Alaska Collection of Z.J. Loussac Public Library, Anchorage Municipal Libraries, Anchorage, Alaska.

Allen, June. "Harold Gillam: A tragic final flight, Ketchikan remembers the search." *SitNews* August 2004, <http://www.sitnews.us/JuneAllen/ HaroldGillam/081704_final_flight.html>.

Batzer family memorabilia and photographs.

Collections of the Ketchikan Museums.

Dawson, Don. "The Gillam Crash." Smithsonian Institute Air and Space Museum, GE Lecture Series, 11/03/88 Lecture Presentation.

Dawson, Don. "The Gillam Plane is Missing!" Calendar, January, February, March, April 1993.

Gill, Jim. "The Gillam Plane Crash," *U.S. Coast Guard Stories,* http://www.jacksjoint.com/gillam.html.

Letter to Mr. and Mrs. H.W. Batzer by Joseph Tippets, March 1, 1943.

Logs of the USS *McLane* and the *Tucsan* 232, National Archives, Washington, D.C.

Museum of History and Industry, Seattle, Wa.

Note to Alta by Joseph Tippets, February 2, 1943. [From notebook in his possession.]

Personal journals, family pictures and memorabilia, letters, etcetera, including those of Mildred Hackett, Desla Bennion, and the LDS Church First Presidency.

Records of the Church of Jesus Christ of Latter-day Saints Archives, including the Northwestern States Mission Historical Record, March 7, 1943.

Report of the Civil Aeronautics Board, August 25, 1943 (see Appendix B).

Report of the U.S. Forest Service/The International Group Historical Aircraft Research, August 2004 (see Appendix D).

Tippets, Joseph H. Two taped recordings of his experiences, 1960s.

Tippets, Joseph H. Report of plane crash, transcribed by M. Morrow, Secretary, American Red Cross, February 16, 1943.

U.S. Coast Guard. 1943 Photographs. (Box 97, Alaska Rescue Operations), National Archives II (College Park, MD), Pictures likely taken by photographer, 3rd Class, M. J. Bailey. Joseph Tippets also had a set of the USCG pictures which have been used.

U.S. Coast Guard. "The Coast Guard at War: Transports and Escorts." Historical Section, Public Information Division, U.S. Coast Guard Headquarters, May 1, 1949 (CGC *McLane*).

Wilson, Paul. "Annette Island 1941-1945," *Our Time.*

# Appendix A

Letter written by Joseph Tippets to the parents of Susan Batzer

Anchorage, Alaska
March 1, 1943

Dear Mr. and Mrs. Batzer:

I do hope that you understand the reason for my not having corresponded with you prior to this time. It has been because of my inability to write. It has been my utmost desire since the very moment of Susan's death to write you concerning her last hours and to express the deep admiration of all those who were with her on the fateful day of January 5th.

Inasmuch as I was associated with the Civil Aeronautics Administration, it seemed natural that she and I were to become well acquainted and we felt that we more or less had common interests through our work connections.

I should like first to state that never in my life should I hope to meet a braver, more appreciative and a more understanding woman than was your daughter, Susan. The brief hours that we all spent together were of such a nature that we had time to evaluate ourselves for what we were and the characters of each other due to the strange circumstances we were in.

I am going to write as nearly as my memory will permit the chronological happenings in order that you might have as complete information on her mental attitude as possible prior to her death. At 11:30 on the morning of January 5th, Susan and Mr. Rich of the CAA called for me at the Olympic Hotel, Seattle and we proceeded to the airport, Boeing Field, from which location we had arranged for passage in the Morrison-Knudsen Lockheed-Electra airplane. Susan was greatly thrilled and overjoyed at the prospect of flying to the north. She realized that it was an adventure of the first order and that flying over such beautiful, yet treacherous, country was something that few have the privilege of doing. Upon our arrival at the airport, there were some delays prior to departure caused by baggage inspection by the immigration authorities and other routine business which always goes be-

fore a flight to the Territory. After the baggage inspection, Susan, Mr. Rich
and myself went to the lunch counter and had a coca-cola and a sandwich.
We returned to the Immigration Building and visited until we were told to
board the airplane.

I should like here to mention that the airplane in which we flew was one
of the latest in design and type and well-equipped and of a similar type used
by airlines in the continental United States. The pilot, Harold Gillam, is considered one of the finest pilots that aviation has ever produced. We boarded
the plane and took off in routine fashion headed for Alaska. Susan sat in the
second seat on the right hand side of the airplane and I was in the last seat
on the right hand side of the airplane. Mr. Cutting sat directly behind Susan,
and Mr. Metzdorf behind Mr. Cutting, and myself behind Mr. Metzdorf.
Numerous times during the eventful trip, I walked up and sat to the side of
Susan and visited with her and pointed out the highlights of the country we
were passing over and discussing generally what she would find in Anchorage
and during these three hours we became very well acquainted.

The technicalities involving the crash, of course, have been published in
detail in the newspapers and are more or less valueless at a time like this. I
should like you to know, however, that among other things, we were caught
in a tremendous storm, the consequence of which resulted in our crashing on
the mountain. Immediately upon our crash, I feel certain that all were temporarily unconscious with the exception of myself. However, within a very few
moments we were talking among ourselves as we had all survived the crash.
We were some minutes getting to Susan as she had been forced into a close
corner and was covered as were the rest of us with baggage. We realized immediately that her hand had been pinned to a part of the ship inside by a part
which had been bent in from the outside of the plane. As to how seriously her
arm was damaged we were unable to ascertain for some time. Mr. Cutting
and myself immediately uncovered her and started frantically to release her
from her pinned position. It was probably 15 to 20 minutes before we were
even able to tell that her hand had been practically severed in the original
crack-up. After a short time, Mr. Cutting's injuries required that he lay down
and Mr. Gillam and myself continued to try and release her. A total of about
two hours were taken before we could accomplish this. In the meantime,

we had put a tourniquet on her shoulder to prevent further loss of blood. However, physicians have informed me that she probably lost sufficient blood before we had even got to her which would have cost her life.

After releasing Susan, we placed her in the rear part of the plane as by this time we definitely knew the airplane would not catch fire. We made her as comfortable as possible by placing seat cushions under her and blankets and coats over her. During the time we were releasing her, she was very cheerful and never lost consciousness and constantly offered suggestions as to what we might do to expedite her release and she was always inquiring as to the condition of the remainder of the people and demanded that they, too, be given some attention. It was very pleasing to know that she was far from being selfish. I feel that she knew her condition was precarious and she wanted others to be looked after as well as herself to preserve as many lives as might be possible. As soon as we were able, we warmed water and fed her bouillon cube soup to warm her. I sat all during the first night caring for the tourniquet on her arm and talking to her. During this time she expressed many words of pleasure about her folks and her aunt which appeared she had only recently been visiting. She also expressed her belief in God and her desire to do what was right as nearly as she had been able. During the rest of the day and the next night I continued to care for her with relatively little change in condition except at times she became slightly irrational. We also realized by this time that it would be impossible for her to survive and all the passengers did all in their power to make her last days or last hours, whichever it might be, as comfortable and as happy as possible. It must be remembered that during these days, it was raining and snowing and the conditions under which we were living were extremely difficult. We managed to keep Susan dry and in as a comfortable position as humanly possible. During Wednesday night, she complained frequently of cold feet. The hot water bottle that she had in her baggage was used to little or no avail. So during this night, I sat on a seat cushion with my bare feet on hers in order that she might keep warm. Early Thursday morning, she became slightly irrational at times and talked of many things of which I did not understand, mostly of individuals and places she had been and happenings throughout her life which, apparently, had influenced her most. She made me promise should she survive, that we would take her to Seattle at which place a friend of hers knew of a good bone specialist whom she desired to care for her hand. Many, many little conversations were held of which my memory does not recall some of the subjects.

At noon of this day, while I was up under the wing of the plane preparing soup for she and Mr. Cutting, Mr. Cutting moved down next to her to care for her while I assisted with other camp operations. At 6:30 that evening, Mr. Cutting called that she had passed away without any further suffering.

We covered her well to protect her from the weather in order that she might lie in comparative peaceful rest and position.

It is very difficult, of course, to write a letter of this kind, but I am sure you would want to know as much of the details as possible. It is hard for we, as mortals, to understand why our young people are taken in the prime of life. Yet, for those of us who believe in the eternity of mankind, we know that many souls are passing from day to day who have not had the proper light and belief in their lives. Therefore, it appears that at certain times the Lord needs young, strong souls returned to Him to act as teachers and instructors to those individuals who are not so fortunate.

Mrs. Tippets and myself expect to arrive in Seattle in the very near future and, if at all possible, we are going to visit you as soon as we can.

I do hope you will forgive this letter being typewritten as my fingers still do not permit me to write in a legible manner. I am going to take the liberty of sending a copy of this letter to Susan's aunt who lives in Camas of whom she spoke so much.

Again, let me express the deepest sympathy and understanding of all those aboard the airplane, Mr. Gebo, Mr. Cutting, Mr. Metzdorf and myself, for the loss of your lovely daughter. May God bless you with the understanding of your loss at this time and buoy you up in this time of sorrow that you might look forth to a brighter future and to that time when we shall all be united and again have the privilege of associating with our loved ones who have gone before us.

*JOSEPH H. TIPPETS (signed)*

# APPENDIX B

Excerpts from the Report of the Civil Aeronautics Board,
dated August 25, 1943 (File No. 1299-43)

Investigation of an accident which occurred on January 5, 1943, at approximately 6:30 p.m. on a heavily timbered mountainside, about 30 miles east of Ketchikan, Alaska. At an elevation of approximately 2,400 feet above sea level, the accident resulted in critical injuries to Miss Susan Winch Batzer, which proved fatal about 48 hours later for lack of medical attention. Robert Gebo and Dewey Metzdorf were seriously injured, while Joseph H. Tippets and Percy Cutting received minor injuries.

Gillam held a commercial pilot certificate with single- and multi-engine 150-265 h.p., land, sea and instrument ratings, and had accumulated approximately 7,412 hours of flying time, about 757 of which were in the type of aircraft involved. Pilot Gillam obtained clearance for a cross-country flight from Boeing Field, Seattle, Washington to Annette Island, Alaska, and after receiving weather data, took off at approximately 1:27 p.m. He plotted his course to follow the Victoria leg of the Seattle Range.

The flight proceeded intact under broken clouds at an altitude of from 3,000 to 3,500 feet. After passing over Victoria, about 30 minutes after takeoff, the pilot laid course along the east side of Vancouver Island and climbed to an altitude of approximately 9,000 feet and over the broken clouds. At about 6:35 p.m. Copilot Gebo computed the speed and estimated their position to be 30 or 40 miles from Annette Island, their destination. At an altitude of approximately 7,000 feet, the left engine stopped. Pilot Gillam called Ketchikan radio and advised them that their left engine had failed and he thought they were in trouble. About this time, a violent downdraft caught the aircraft and the pilot became so busy in an attempt to recover normal flight attitude that further effort to communicate with Ketchikan by radio was abandoned. The plane broke out of a ragged overcast at an elevation of 2,500 feet, headed in a northerly direction and parallel to a ridge of mountains. There were other mountains ahead. Gillam turned off the right engine, headed toward a clearing on the side of the mountain, and pulled the plane up into a stalled attitude for a crash landing. The right wing contacted and sheared two tall trees at mid-height, and the plane swerved to the right about 90°, struck the ground on the stub of a broken right wing and bottom of the fuse-lage, and stopped in an upright position.

The four survivors remained lost for a period of 29 days following the accident, during which time an extensive air, land, and water search was carried on over large areas east and south of Ketchikan and up into British Columbia. After continuing the hazardous search during the winter weather for a period of approximately three weeks, the party was given up for lost and the search was abandoned.

Pilot Harold Gillam was apparently uninjured in the accident but, in an effort to summon aid to his injured passengers, he perished by exposure and freezing. His remains were found on February 6, 1943, on the shores of the Boca de Quadra Inlet, approximately 7 miles from the scene of the accident.

Investigation revealed that Gillam had consulted personnel of the Weather Bureau at Boeing Field prior to his departure. He studied the surface and winds aloft charts, the hourly reports and Pan American Airways spot weather reports, and was advised that the overcast condition extended over the coastal route with occasional breaks in the lower layers, occasional light rains and moderate icing and precipitation. After deciding to take the coastal route, he was again cautioned about icing conditions to be expected in clouds. He was informed that winds aloft would be around 270°, with velocities of 30 to 40 m.p.h. above 6,000 feet and reduced velocities at lower levels. He was offered a copy of the United States and Alaska codes for obtaining weather, which he declined, remarking that if he needed further weather data, he would declare an emergency and get the report in the clear.

The Fraser River Aeronautical Chart being used by Pilot Gillam, and which was recovered from the wreckage, was out of date and showed the Annette Island Radio Range incorrectly.

No attempt was made en route to contact the ground stations by radio to verify the Annette Island range headings or to report the progress of the flight. Radio reception was good, according to Gebo, and their radio transmission was subsequently reported by the Army Control Tower at Annette Island as satisfactory. It is quite evident that Gillam and Gebo were, at least temporarily, lost. According to Gebo, both were confused by the radio range signals they were receiving and Gillam was preparing to use his radio direction finder equipment at the time the left engine stopped. They had not used their direction finder equipment to establish their track or position at any time during the flight, nor had they reported their position since leaving Seattle, which made the unsuccessful search more difficult.

While the stoppage of the left engine from an undetermined cause in extremely rough weather and over hazardous terrain undoubtedly was the primary cause of the accident, it is apparent that strong contributing factors were the pilot's failure (1) to equip himself with an up-to-date aeronautical chart and (2) to utilize the radio aids available to him to accurately establish the position of the flight while on instruments.

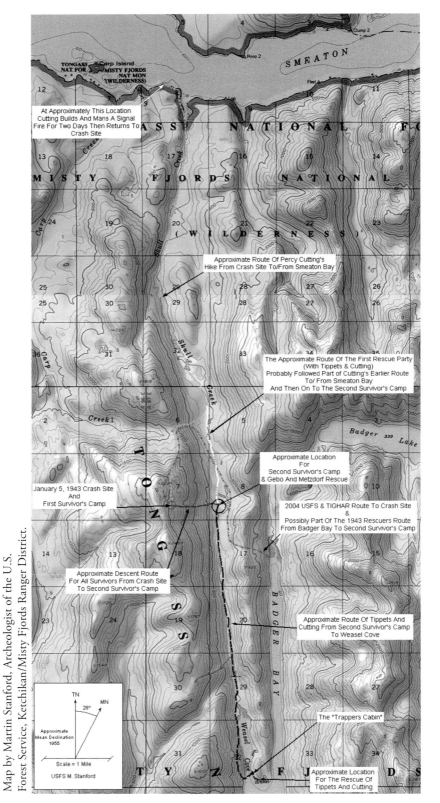

At Approximately This Location Cutting Builds And Mans A Signal Fire For Two Days Then Returns To Crash Site

Approximate Route Of Percy Cutting's Hike From Crash Site To/From Smeaton Bay

The Approximate Route Of The First Rescue Party (With Tippets & Cutting) Probably Followed Part of Cutting's Earlier Route To/ From Smeaton Bay And Then On To The Second Survivor's Camp

Approximate Location For Second Survivor's Camp & Gebo And Metzdorf Rescue

January 5, 1943 Crash Site And First Survivor's Camp

2004 USFS & TIGHAR Route To Crash Site & Possibly Part Of The 1943 Rescuers Route From Badger Bay To Second Survivor's Camp

Approximate Descent Route For All Survivors From Crash Site To Second Survivor's Camp

Approximate Route Of Tippets And Cutting From Second Survivor's Camp To Weasel Cove

The "Trappers Cabin"

Approximate Location For The Rescue Of Tippets And Cutting

TN  MN
28°

Approximate Mean Declination 1955

Scale = 1 Mile

USFS M. Stanford

Map by Martin Stanford, Archeologist of the U.S. Forest Service, Ketchikan/Misty Fjords Ranger District.

128

# Appendix C

## New Guidelines for Equipment and Supplies to be Carried on Commercial Aircraft Flying over Wilderness Areas, 1943

In the weeks following the recovery of the Morrison-Knudsen NC14915 survivors, there is an exchange between the U.S. Department of the Interior, the governor of the Alaska Territory (Ernest Gruening), and Canadian government parties. A list is established of emergency equipment and supplies that should be carried on planes in the region (see below):

Commercial aircraft which are operating in unsettled or sparsely settled areas must carry the following emergency equipment required for air worthiness.

1. Not less than five pounds of concentrated food or its equivalent in ordinary foods on board the aircraft at the time of leaving the base. This food shall be packed in a waterproof package or container and shall be inspected once in every six months to make certain that it is good. Certification of this inspection shall be made by the operator on a tag or label affixed to the package.

2. Adequate cooking utensils and mess tins.

3. Matches in waterproof container.

4. Pocket compass.

5. Three-quarter size ax with 28-inch handle.

6. Snare wire, 4 ounces.

Additional summer equipment:

7. Sufficient mosquito bars or fly proof tent to protect occupants of the aircraft.

8. Four trawls, two lines and sinkers.

9. One fish net.

Additional winter equipment:
10. Sufficient sleeping bags for occupants of aircraft.
11. At least two pairs of snow shoes.

Provision on the above scale must be made for any additional passengers expected before the aircraft returns to its base.

It should be noted that the operator is expected to use his judgement in making further additions to the above list in the occasion of exceptionally long flights away from the base.

The following suggestions are made:

Item 1 – Care should be taken to obtain foods of high nutritive value that are not subject to damage by heat or cold. It has been found preferable to carry only the simplest foods, such as Pemmican and an easily prepared cereal rather than the more complex preparations now on the market.

Item 3 – A few matches in paraffin cases may be conveniently packed in every package of concentrated food but to avoid confusion a separate supply should also be carried.

Item 4 – Marching compass is preferable.

Item 6 – Four-pound ax is most serviceable.

Item 9 – A two-inch mesh is suggested by one experienced operator.

Item 10 – It is not considered necessary to provide a sleeping bag for each passenger; probably two large button type sleeping bags would provide protection for six persons in an emergency.

A pack sack is desirable and serves as a handy container for the smaller items.

The provision of fire arms is a matter which must be decided by the operator and it's not intended to lay down a rule owing to the varying conditions in different parts of the country.

# APPENDIX D

## USFS/TIGHAR Site Examination – 2004

In August of 2004, a joint group of U.S. Forest Service personnel (Ketchikan/Misty Fjords Ranger District, Tongass National Forest, Alaska) and members of the International Group for Historic Aircraft Recovery (TIGHAR) visited and conducted a thorough survey of the Harold Gillam Lockheed Electra airplane crash site.

USFS/TIGHAR – 2004

*"As an airways engineer with the Civil Aeronautics Administration, I have been present at the scene of many airplane crashes. I can honestly say that I have never seen a plane in the condition ours was in and known anyone to survive." Joseph Tippets*

*Excerpts from their report:*

From August 2 to 5, 2004, a seven-person team composed of members of the International Group for Historic Aircraft Recovery

(TIGHAR) and personnel from the Ketchikan/Misty Fjords Ranger District of the Tongass National Forest re-located the wreck site and briefly documented its character by surface survey. Several artifacts were recovered from the site for study purposes with the permission of the United States Forest Service (USFS). This is the report of the TIGHAR's archaeological fieldwork.

Descriptions and other survivor accounts indicated that there was no post crash fire, and that the fuselage of the aircraft may have been sufficiently well preserved to retain intact dados if present. These accounts, and a map drawn by local aviation enthusiast Don "Bucky"

USFS/TIGHAR – 2004

*Crash remains*

Dawson, provided enough location details to allow Forest Service personnel to re-locate the crash site by air reconnaissance on July 27, 2004. Global Positioning Satellite (GPS) coordinates were obtained during the flyover that would prove essential to locating wreckage on foot in the densely wooded environment.

Following a heading toward the GPS coordinates established by a flyover the previous week, the wreckage was located late in the afternoon of August 3. Due to the late hour of the arrival at the crash site, the team performed an initial inspection of the area, which revealed the wreckage remained tightly concentrated along a steep drainage.

All major aircraft components appeared present except for the engines, propellers, control wheels and rudders.

On the next morning of August 4, all participants returned to the wreckage site and commenced survey, documentation, and sampling duties. They identified, measured, photographed, and then carefully removed 16 artifacts from the wreckage after they had been reconciled to the baseline for the location.

The wreckage is concentrated between 1,737 feet and 1,689 feet elevation. It is distributed for 19 linear meters along a narrow (less than 1 m), steep drainage that runs east-northeast down to a muskeg valley. This drainage, running through metamorphic rubble over a series of rock outcrops and logs forming small waterfalls, is continually filled with varying levels of water in warmer months due to the temperate rain forest environment. Winter snowfall averages 32 inches in Ketchikan with annual rainfall totaling132 inches. Pooling water levels were 5 cm or less and water was cascading over a small section of the wreckage during our survey. The sides of the drainage are equally steep and densely forested with both mountain and western hemlock, Sitka spruce, and knee- to waist-high understory vegetation. The primary wreckage concentration includes the bottom of the instrument panel and controls (sans wheels), cockpit, bulkhead and cockpit door, auxiliary fuel tank, left wing, partial right wing (inverted with exposed landing gear retracted) cowling sections, torn fuselage sections, empennage (sans rudders), and the severed outboard right wing section (inverted). Post crash damage over time has resulted from compression by snowfall, impact by deadfall, and salvage efforts.

The fuselage area is particularly compromised. Most of the roof and sides of the fuselage have been separated from the deck. Much of the fuselage behind station 239 is crushed and hidden from view under the inverted right wing section. This wing was inverted during the removal of the right engine. Overall, it appears the entire debris field has moved very little since the time of the accident.

Of note among the remnants of the fuselage is the aluminum auxiliary fuel tank. It is similar to the auxiliary tanks known to have been mounted in the Earhart Electra. Still structurally sound with steel bands securing it to the floor, the tank sustained only moderate damage. The tank's mounting bands were carefully cut, and the tank was moved to allow for the removal of dado-like objects for laboratory examination. The tank was then replaced as found.

A pair of c.1940 women's shoes was found in the exposed fuselage section. These shoes most likely belonged to Susan Batzer, the young stenographer employed by Morrison-Knudsen* who expired 48 hours after the accident from injuries sustained in the crash landing. Ms. Batzer's* body was recovered several weeks after the survivors were rescued.

Very little wreckage is apparent on the slopes above the streambed. Exceptions include a section of engine cowling 13 meters north/ northwest of the baseline at 21 meters down from the datum, and two engine cylinders with one oil cooler 10 meters south/southeast of the baseline at 18 meters down from the datum. The overall absence of engine components reflects the known removal of the right engine for exhibition in the Pioneer Air Museum of Fairbanks and the propensity for engines to separate from the nacelles upon impact with terrain.

An additional concentration of artifacts appears to be the remains of an improvised latrine established by the wreck's survivors, located 19 meters south/southwest of the baseline at 30 meters down from the datum point. The latrine area contains the toilet seat and aluminum chamber pot from the aircraft lavatory, as well as the remnants of a tin can.

Despite the crash landing, over 60 years of heavy snowfall and continuing water flow, salvage operations and possibly some looting activity, most of the aircraft remains intact although significantly damaged. The left wing exhibits the faded USA flying flag insignia required for all civilian aircraft operating in Alaskan airspace during World War II.

### Interpretation

The location and condition of the wreckage is consistent with contemporary accounts of the crash landing by survivors. Lockheed

*Miss Batzer was a new CAA employee.

Electra aircraft wrecks that were not consumed by post crash fires are extremely rare. Save for absence of some components, most notably the engines, propellers, rudders, and control wheels, and the inverted position of the right wing and resulting crushed fuselage, NC14915 lies in situ most likely where it came to rest on January 5, 1943.

In the 1980s, salvagers in association with the Tongass Historical society visited the site to recover artifacts for preservation and exhibition. One engine cylinder and the right rudder were recovered in 1981. The right engine, complete with its propeller, and left rudder (now on exhibit at the Pioneer Air Museum in Fairbanks) were recovered in 1984 by helicopter airlift.

The left engine, although unknown at the time of this survey, remains buried on the south side of the drainage just forward of the left wing. While two cylinders, one oil cooler, and two sections of exhaust manifold from an engine were located during the survey, no other engine parts were noted. The extremely rugged terrain, dense forest, and limited time available on site did not allow for the investigation of a larger area in which additional artifacts might be recorded. Neither could the initial impact site be ascertained due to these limitations.

The rudders and three of the four propeller blades are currently in the possession of Randy Acord of the Pioneer Air Museum in Fairbanks and Don "Bucky" Dawson of Ketchikan, being held for the Tongass Historical Society. The right engine propeller is complete and remains attached to the engine, now on exhibit in Fairbanks. Mr. Dawson, who has visited the wreckage on five occasions and participated in the salvage operations, has informed TIGHAR that he is storing one cylinder and one propeller blade from the left engine for the Tongass Historical Society, and that the other propeller blade remains at the wreck site. The TIGHAR/USFS survey team was unable to locate this remaining blade in situ.

The missing control wheels are most likely the result of previous salvage or looting. Mr. Dawson indicated that the wheels were missing at the time of his first visit to the site. In the summer of 1943, a salvage crew from Ellis Airlines visited the wreckage and obtained usable engine parts, a radio, and flight instruments. Others have visited the site over the years, motivated to the arduous trek by need for parts, want of souvenirs, or curiosity.

Both TIGHAR and the United States Forest Service agree that the exact location of the wreckage must be kept strictly confidential in order to protect the site from additional salvage or looting. Thus, this report contains no GPS coordinates or anything other than a general description of the area. While remote and in rugged wilderness country, it is possible that curious seekers visiting the site may cause further loss of integrity. Since the designation of Misty Fjords as a National Wilderness Area, helicopters are not allowed to land in the area, thus challenging the unauthorized recovery of major wreckage components.

### Eligibility for the National Register of Historic Places

In its proposal to the United States Forest Service to conduct this survey, TIGHAR offered the opinion that the Gillam crash site is eligible for the National Register of Historic Places. We believe such eligibility is appropriate under National Register criteria "a" for association with aviation (particularly Alaska aviation) history and "d" as a source of useful historical information including, but not limited to, the information that TIGHAR seeks in connection with testing the Nikumaroro Hypothesis for Amelia Earhart's disappearance.

Archaeologists John Autrey and Martin Stanford of the Ketchikan/ Misty Fjords Ranger District, Tongass National Forest, submitted a determination of eligibility report (CRM Report 20041005520008) to the State Historic Preservation Officer (SHPO) of Alaska. Within this report, Autrey and Stanford asserted that the Gillam crash site, 49-KET-00910, was eligible for the National Register of Historic Places under criteria "b" for its association with Harold Gillam, and "d" as a source for information that may answer research questions from the Nikumaroro Hypothesis for Amelia Earhart's disappearance. Unfortunately the Alaska SHPO disagreed with TIGHAR and the National Forest Service.

**Appendix 2: Lockheed Electra**

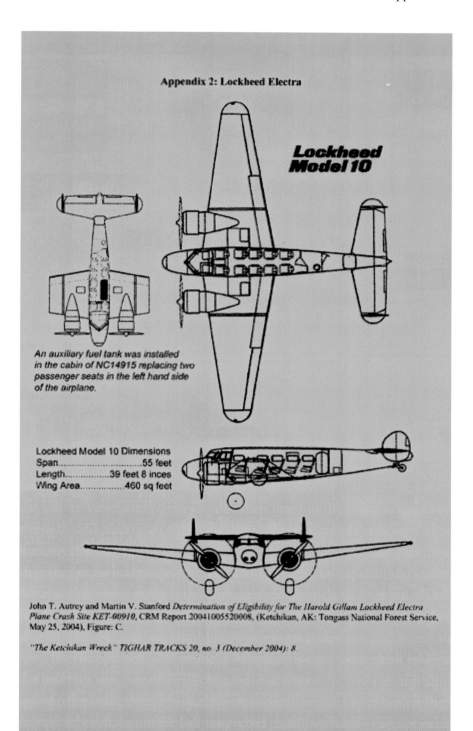

*An auxiliary fuel tank was installed in the cabin of NC14915 replacing two passenger seats in the left hand side of the airplane.*

Lockheed Model 10 Dimensions
Span.................................55 feet
Length................39 feet 8 inces
Wing Area................460 sq feet

John T. Autrey and Martin V. Stanford *Determination of Eligibility for The Harold Gillam Lockheed Electra Plane Crash Site KET-00910*, CRM Report 20041005520008, (Ketchikan, AK: Tongass National Forest Service, May 25, 2004), Figure: C.

*"The Ketchikan Wreck" TIGHAR TRACKS 20, no. 3 (December 2004): 8.*

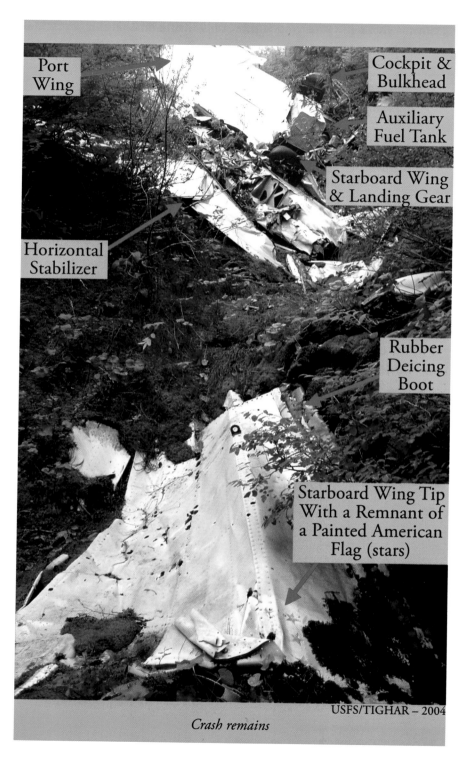

Port Wing

Cockpit & Bulkhead

Auxiliary Fuel Tank

Starboard Wing & Landing Gear

Horizontal Stabilizer

Rubber Deicing Boot

Starboard Wing Tip With a Remnant of a Painted American Flag (stars)

USFS/TIGHAR – 2004

*Crash remains*

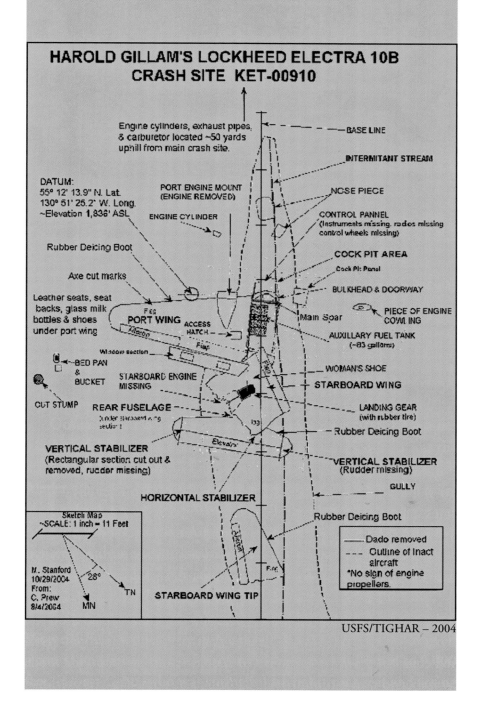

USFS/TIGHAR – 2004

USFS/TIGHAR – 2004

*KET-910 Gillam's Lockheed Electra 10-B Control Panel*

Nose Pieces

Woman's Shoe

USFS/TIGHAR – 2004

Bulkhead-Blue Colored Wash

Cockpit & Control Panel

Wood Paneling & Veneer

Doorway & Door Frame

Auxiliary Fuel Tank

Main Wing Spar

Leather Seat Cover

USFS/TIGHAR – 2004

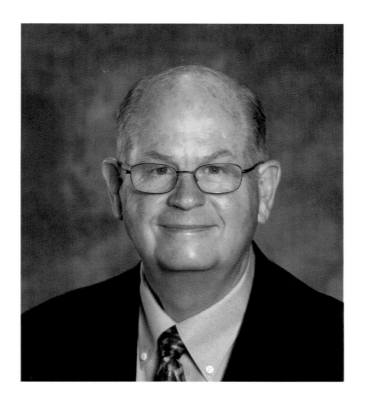

About the Author
## John M. Tippets

John is a proud Alaskan, born in Providence Hospital at Anchorage in 1941. His early years were spent in Alaska and the Washington, D.C. area where his Dad worked for the government. After two years serving as a church missionary in Eastern Canada, he received his Bachelor's and MBA degrees from the University of California at Los Angeles. Always interested in aviation, John began his career with American Airlines while still in college. He will retire in June, 2008 after 42 years associated with the airline. He is currently CEO of the American Airlines Federal Credit Union.

His quest to research and write about the lives of his parents developed from a wish to share their stories with his children and grandchildren. *Hearts of Courage* attempts to capture the strong faith of Joseph and Alta Tippets and bring to life how their prayers were miraculously answered in January and February, 1943.

John and his wife, Bonnie, live in Colleyville, Texas.

More information about Harold Gillam, the Electra's pilot, may be found in Arnold Griese's book, *Bush Pilot*.